A-level
In a Week

Biology

Year 2

Eliot
Attridge

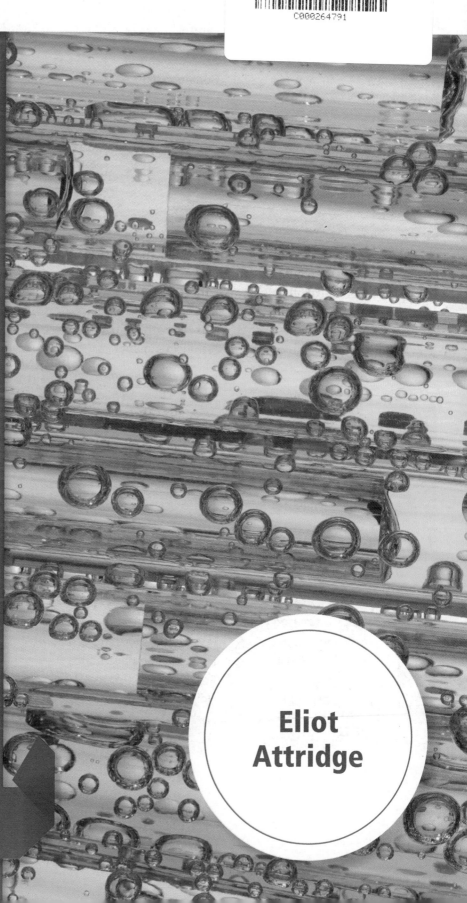

CONTENTS

DAY 1

Page	Estimated time	Topic	Date	Time taken	Completed
4	40 minutes	Cell Signalling			☐
8	40 minutes	Homeostasis			☐
12	40 minutes	Excretion			☐
16	40 minutes	The Kidney			☐

DAY 2

Page	Estimated time	Topic	Date	Time taken	Completed
20	40 minutes	Nervous Communication			☐
24	40 minutes	Electrical Signals			☐
28	40 minutes	Endocrine System			☐
32	40 minutes	Control of Blood Glucose			☐
36	40 minutes	Plant Growth Regulators			☐
40	40 minutes	Plant Experiments			☐

DAY 3

Page	Estimated time	Topic	Date	Time taken	Completed
44	40 minutes	Nervous System Organisation			☐
48	40 minutes	Muscle Action			☐
52	40 minutes	Skeletal Tissues			☐
56	40 minutes	The Skeleton			☐

DAY 4

Page	Estimated time	Topic	Date	Time taken	Completed
60	40 minutes	Photosynthesis			☐
64	40 minutes	Light-Independent Stage			☐
68	40 minutes	Respiration			☐
72	40 minutes	Holoenzymes			☐

DAY 5

Page	Estimated time	Topic	Date	Time taken	Completed
76	40 minutes	Mutations			☐
80	40 minutes	Regulatory Mechanisms			☐
84	40 minutes	Embryonic Development			☐
88	40 minutes	Inheritance			☐

DAY 6

Page	Estimated time	Topic	Date	Time taken	Completed
92	40 minutes	Variation			☐
96	40 minutes	Analysing Experimental Results			☐
100	40 minutes	DNA Sequencing			☐

DAY 7

Page	Estimated time	Topic	Date	Time taken	Completed
104	40 minutes	Genetic Engineering			☐
108	40 minutes	Biotechnology			☐
112	40 minutes	Ecosystems			☐
116	40 minutes	Population Size			☐

120	Answers
134	Index

Cell Signalling

The Need to Communicate

The ability to respond to changes in the environment is one of the characteristics of living things. Even the simplest organisms comprising a single cell (e.g. **prokaryotes**) are able to respond to basic environmental stimuli, such as the presence or absence of a food source. In most single cells the response is based on a gradient of some kind. For example, sperm follow both a thermal gradient that peaks near the released egg and a chemical gradient.

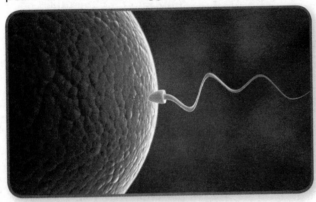

Environmental Changes

With larger multicellular organisms the increase in size reduces the surface area to volume ratio. The organism can no longer rely on the diffusion of a chemical across its cell surface membrane. Instead, organisms have evolved communication systems so that they can better detect and respond to external environmental change.

The increase in the size of an organism also creates issues. When there are many cells there needs to be a way of communicating what is going on in those cells so that the organism's metabolism is coordinated. These are internal environmental changes.

In most instances the environmental change detected is chemical in nature.

Cell Signalling

Studies of how cells communicate have shown that a set of cell-signalling mechanisms appears in most life forms on Earth. This is further evidence that all life shares a common ancestor. Understanding how cells communicate is important as it enables scientists to work out how to influence cells and develop treatments for certain metabolic disorders.

When cells are adjacent to one another communication is through direct contact between cell surface membranes. This type of cell signalling is called **cell recognition**. Cells can also communicate with cells that are close but not in contact, by sending chemicals dissolved in the **cytosol**.

There are two ways that cells can send chemical messages to adjacent cells. The first is through passing the signalling molecules via cell junctions. Cell junctions allow molecules to pass easily between two cells.

Chemical messages can also be sent long distance and read by cells with particular receptors to the signalling chemical. The **endocrine system** in animals is an example of this type of cell signalling, as is the transport of **plant growth regulators** (plant hormones) in plants.

Cell Junctions

In animal cells, a transmembrane protein complex called a **connexon** connects the interior of a cell to the exterior. The connexon of a cell attaches to a corresponding connexon protein on an adjacent cell. This creates a pore connecting the two cells to each other. The pores can be open or closed.

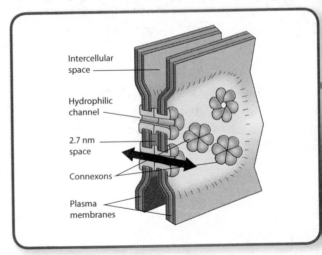

Intercellular space

Hydrophilic channel

2.7 nm space

Connexons

Plasma membranes

In plants, the cell junctions are called **plasmodesmata** and extend from the cell surface membrane through the cell wall.

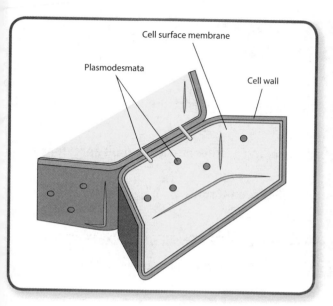

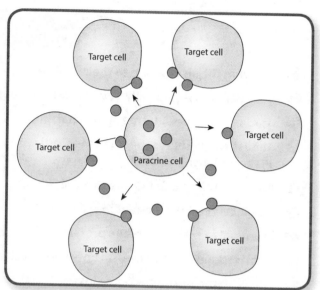

The benefit of the animal cell junctions and plant plasmodesmata is that hydrophilic substances can be passed from one cell to another through the cell surface membrane.

Cell–cell Recognition

Animal cells can also communicate using molecules such as glycoproteins and glycolipids that protrude from the cell surface membrane. The cells have matching receptors that ensure the correct cell pairing.

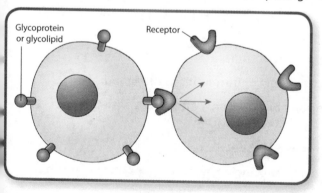

This type of cell recognition is common in the immune system and in embryo development.

Secreted Molecules

Cells can also send signals by secretion of chemicals into the space between cells. The cell releases chemicals that then can be detected by the receiving cells. **Paracrine** signalling is where signalling chemicals, e.g. regulator chemicals such as growth factors, pass to local cells.

Synaptic signalling is where a neurone releases a neurotransmitter into the synapse. The neurotransmitter then stimulates a response in the target, or receiving cell, e.g. an effector cell, or another neurone.

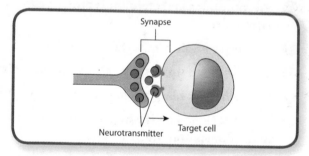

Endocrine signalling involves the long-distance transport of signalling molecules, called hormones, in the blood. Hormones can contact all cells in the body, but only those with receptors will receive and act on the message.

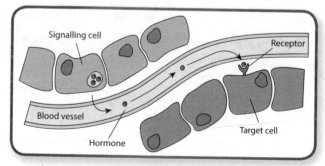

In plants, plant growth regulators (plant hormones) such as auxin are produced in the tip of a shoot. These hormones migrate down the shoot and can produce a response in other cells. Auxin stimulates the growth of target cells.

SUMMARY

- All living things respond to their environment.
- An organism can typically detect changes in a gradient, such as a chemical, thermal or light gradient.
- Gradients can be external or internal.
- Almost all life shares the same mechanisms for cell signalling, suggesting a common ancestor for all life on Earth.
- Adjacent cells communicate through direct contact (cell recognition).
- Chemicals can also be sent in the cytosol.
- In animals a transmembrane protein called a connexon connects the interior of a cell to the exterior.
- A corresponding connexon on an adjacent cell creates a pore that allows substances to flow through.
- The pore can be opened and closed.
- In plants the cell junctions are called plasmodesmata.
- Plasmodesmata extend from the cell surface membrane through the cell wall.
- Cell junctions enable hydrophilic substances to pass between cells.
- Glycoproteins and glycolipids protrude from cell surfaces and can be recognised by receptors on another cell.
- Cell recognition is important in the immune system and in embryo development.
- Cells can send signals over short and long distances to affect other cells.
- Paracrine signalling is where local cells are affected, e.g. by growth factors.
- Synaptic signalling is where a neurone transmits a nerve impulse, resulting in the release of a neurotransmitter into a synapse.
- The neurotransmitter stimulates a response in the effector cell.
- Endocrine signalling involves the long-distance transport of hormones in the blood.
- Hormones come into contact with all cells in the body but they only affect cells with the correct receptors on the surface.
- Plant growth regulators (plant hormones) are produced in specific cells.
- The plant growth regulator travels through the plant, causing an effect (e.g. growth) in another part of the plant.

1. Why are gradients important for detecting changes in the environment?

2. What is cell recognition?

3. What is the purpose of a connexon?

4. What types of molecule protrude from the surface of a cell and are used for cell signalling?

5. What is meant when a molecule is said to be hydrophilic?

6. What are plasmodesmata?

7. Draw a diagram to demonstrate paracrine signalling.

8. What is synaptic signalling?

9. How does endocrine signalling differ from paracrine signalling?

10. What are plant growth regulators?

PRACTICE QUESTIONS

1. Plant and animal cells are able to send signals to other cells. This involves the movement of chemicals.

   a) Describe the cell junctions involved in cell signalling that are present in animal cells. **[2 marks]**

   b) Plant cells have a different method of communication. How does this method allow substances to pass from cell to cell? **[2 marks]**

   c) What does the similarity of the methods used for cell recognition in animals and plants tell scientists about the relatedness of life on Earth? **[1 mark]**

2. a) Describe the similarities and differences between paracrine signalling and synaptic signalling in mammals. **[4 marks]**

   b) What is endocrine signalling? **[2 marks]**

Homeostasis

The ability to maintain a constant internal environment is called **homeostasis**. The environment in which an organism lives is likely to vary, so being able to control the internal environment gives an organism an advantage over those that cannot. The type of homeostasis depends on the substance or condition that needs to be maintained.

Examples in mammals include:

Temperature homeostasis (thermoregulation): this is where internal body temperature is maintained to ensure that metabolic reactions take place under optimal conditions.

pH homeostasis: if the pH of the blood changes then various proteins, such as enzymes, can be structurally altered or denatured.

Glucose homeostasis: levels of glucose have to be maintained within a narrow range. Too little glucose in the blood causes respiration to stop, whereas too much glucose can affect proteins, causing damage. Insulin causes a reduction in blood glucose concentration, whereas other chemicals, such as glucagon, increase it.

Fluid homeostasis: levels of fluids in the body are kept constant by regulating the amount of water. The kidneys can actively reabsorb water if the body needs to reduce water loss.

Regulation

To effectively carry out homeostasis there has to be communication between the different cells in the body. The cells that detect the change from the normal state are called **receptor cells**. Receptor cells send a signal to a **control centre**, which processes the information from the receptor cells and instigates a response. The control centre sends a signal to **effectors**, which carry out the required response.

Receptor Cells

Receptor cells are found throughout the body. Receptors are cells that detect an environmental change, such as temperature, light, pH or water level. They are specialised cells that are connected to the control centre via neurones. The neurones transmit an electrical signal when the environmental stimulus exceeds a certain threshold.

The Control Centre

In most instances the control centre of an animal is its brain. The brain is a complex organ that processes the information from the different receptors and initiates a response. If the brain gets damaged then the responses can stop and homeostasis will fail.

Effectors

There are two types of cell that can respond during homeostasis. As they are responsible for the *effect* they are called effectors. Muscle cells can be instructed to carry out a motor response by contracting or relaxing. Glands can secrete or stop secreting chemical messages.

Negative Feedback

If the temperature of an organism grows too high, then the organism needs to reduce its temperature. Conditions are brought back to a set level if they have deviated from that level. This is an example of negative feedback. The response causes a change in the opposite direction to the original deviation from normal.

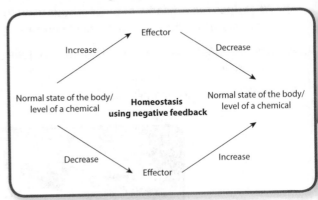

Positive Feedback

During positive feedback the response to a signal does not *reduce* the change from the normal but instead *increases* it further. One example is childbirth, when contractions start in response to the release of a hormone called oxytocin into the bloodstream from the pituitary gland in the brain (the control centre). The contractions are detected by receptors in the uterus and cervix, which feed back to the brain to release more oxytocin. This causes more contractions to occur, and so on. The contractions increase in strength and frequency until the baby is born and the cycle stops.

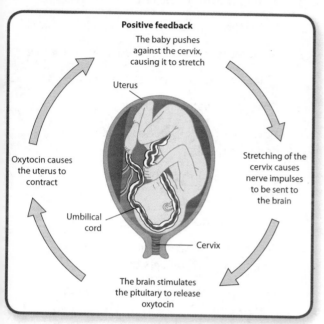

Positive feedback

The baby pushes against the cervix, causing it to stretch

Uterus

Oxytocin causes the uterus to contract

Stretching of the cervix causes nerve impulses to be sent to the brain

Umbilical cord

Cervix

The brain stimulates the pituitary to release oxytocin

Another example of positive feedback in the body is the process of blood clotting after injury. At the site of a wound such as a graze platelets start to build up and release chemicals to attract more platelets. The platelets continue to accumulate and release chemicals until a clot is formed and the wound sealed.

Poikilothermy and Homeothermy

Poikilothermic organisms have a body temperature that varies with the external environment. Most animals other than birds and mammals are poikilothermic.

Homeothermic organisms have a body temperature that remains constant, despite the outside temperature. Birds and mammals fit into this group. Some reptiles, large fish and insects are partially homeothermic as they are able to maintain a body temperature that is different from the external environment.

Ectothermy and Endothermy

Organisms need to maintain their internal temperature. Animals such as invertebrates and vertebrates such as reptiles and amphibians and most fish are **ectotherms**. Although metabolic reactions inside an ectotherm's body produce some heat, this is so little as to be negligible compared

to environmental changes in temperature. If an ectotherm needs to cool down it has to move somewhere cooler. If it is not warm enough, it has to move closer to a source of heat. The response is behavioural. In the past ectodermal vertebrates were referred to as being 'cold blooded'. This is not correct, however. Ectotherms typically have a slower metabolic rate and require less energy to survive. Note that an ectothermic animal is not necessarily poikilothermic.

Endotherms are organisms that can use the heat liberated in metabolic reactions to keep the body warm, rather than relying on external sources of heat. The only animal groups in which every member of the group is an endotherm are the birds and mammals. Endothermy requires a lot of energy to generate the heat, so endotherms require a high-energy diet and often have to spend their time eating or finding food.

Temperature Control

Endotherms have temperature receptors in the skin. These are called peripheral temperature receptors. There are two types of peripheral temperature receptor: those that can detect low temperatures in the immediate vicinity and those that can detect high temperatures.

The signals from both sets of receptors are sent via neurones to the brain. The hypothalamus is the part of the brain that regulates body temperature. The hypothalamic thermoregulatory centre analyses the information from all of the receptors and initiates a response if there is a deviation from the normal temperature. The signal from the hypothalamus is sent via neurones to effectors, which carry out the appropriate response.

High Temperature

If the temperature is too high then one of the effectors will be sweat glands, which will produce sweat. The evaporation of sweat removes some of the excess heat from the body, cooling it down. In addition, shunt vessels in the arterioles leading to capillary beds close to the skin surface are opened (vasodilation; see figure overleaf). This enables blood to flow closer to the surface of the skin, allowing heat to be released.

Low Temperature

If the temperature is too low, one of the effectors will be muscles attached to the hairs in the skin. These cause hairs to stand up, trapping a layer of air for insulation.

The muscles can also be stimulated to start contracting and relaxing, which is observed as the process of shivering. This muscle activity causes extra heat to be produced from respiration. In addition, shunt vessels in the arterioles leading to capillary beds close to the skin surface are closed, causing the blood to flow deeper in the body (vasoconstriction). The skin gets paler and less heat is lost from the blood.

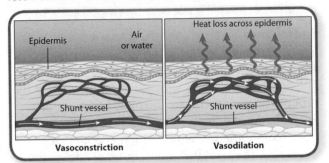

Vasoconstriction   Vasodilation

Although endotherms can regulate internal body temperature, they also use behavioural responses to change temperature. For example, they may seek shade to escape hot sun, enter water or rest rather than moving. When food is scarce and external temperatures are low they may even sleep for long periods (hibernation) to reduce energy costs.

QUICK TEST

1. What is meant by the term homeostasis?

2. Name three types of homeostasis in mammals.

3. What is the main control centre in an animal?

4. What are the two types of effector?

5. Describe negative feedback.

6. How does positive feedback differ from negative feedback?

7. How is childbirth an example of positive feedback?

8. What are endotherms and ectotherms?

9. Describe what happens to an endotherm when temperature gets too low.

10. Why do ectotherms require less energy than endotherms?

SUMMARY

- Homeostasis is the ability to maintain a constant internal environment.

- The ability to carry out homeostasis confers an advantage over those that cannot.

- There are many types of homeostatic control, e.g. of temperature, pH, fluids.

- Homeostasis relies on receptors, a control centre and effectors.

- Receptor cells are specialised cells that detect a change in a stimulus (e.g. light, temperature, pH, water level).

- The control centre in an animal is the brain, a complex organ that processes information from receptor cells and initiates a response.

- There are two types of effector: muscles and glands.

- Negative feedback is the main way that organisms maintain homeostasis. A change from normal initiates a response that causes a corrective response by a control centre in the opposite direction to the change.

- An example of negative feedback is reducing body temperature if it becomes too high. If the temperature is too low, the correction response is to increase temperature.

- Positive feedback is where a receptor cell detects a signal and the response of the control centre is to increase the signal further. One example is childbirth. Contractions start when the hormone oxytocin is released; contractions cause more oxytocin to be released, which increases the strength and frequency of contractions until the baby is born.

- Ectotherms (such as reptiles and invertebrates) produce only a small amount of heat through metabolic reactions, so raising body temperature requires a behavioural response, with the organism moving closer to a heat source. Ectotherms require less energy to survive.

- Endotherms (such as birds and mammals) can use the heat produced through metabolism to keep warm. They require a lot of energy to maintain body temperature.

- Peripheral temperature receptors in the skin detect either cold or warm conditions.

- The thermoregulatory centre in the hypothalamus receives nervous impulses from the receptors and coordinates the response via messages to the effectors.

- With high temperatures, sweat glands produce sweat and shunt vessels in the arterioles are opened (vasodilation), enabling blood to flow closer to the skin surface, thus allowing heat to leave the body more effectively.

- With cold temperatures, muscles attached to skin hairs cause them to stand up, trapping a layer of air for insulation. The muscles also contract and relax, causing shivering, which generates more heat. Shunt vessels close, causing blood to flow deeper in the body, conserving heat.

PRACTICE QUESTIONS

1. The opah (*Lampris guttatus*) was the first completely endothermic fish to be discovered. It spends most of its time at least 45 m below the ocean surface. Animals such as the opah can be put into categories dependent upon how they obtain their body heat.

a) What is the name of the process governing body temperature? **[1 mark]**

b) Using your knowledge, suggest what advantage the opah would have compared to other fish. **[2 marks]**

c) Poikilothermic ectotherms are restricted to temperatures below 40°C. Why is this so? **[1 mark]**

Excretion

Not all of the products of a metabolic reaction are useful. Those that cannot be used or stored safely, or are in excess, can be classified as being waste products. All living things have to remove waste products as they will alter the internal environment, upsetting the homeostatic balance.

Removal of waste can be seen as a negative feedback mechanism. An increase in waste leads to excretion to remove the waste.

Note that **excretion** is the removal of metabolic waste from the organism whereas **egestion** is the process of discharging non-digested material from a cell or organism, i.e. defacating.

Respiration

The purpose of respiration is to liberate energy from food. The aerobic respiration of glucose leads to the products water and carbon dioxide:

$$C_6H_{12}O_6 \; + \; 6O_2 \; \rightarrow \; 6H_2O \; + \; 6CO_2$$

Glucose oxygen water carbon dioxide

Water produced through respiration can be used in other metabolic reactions, such as hydrolysis of proteins into amino acids. Typically some water will be removed via the lungs (see figure). Air breathed out (exhaled) contains more water than air breathed in (inhaled).

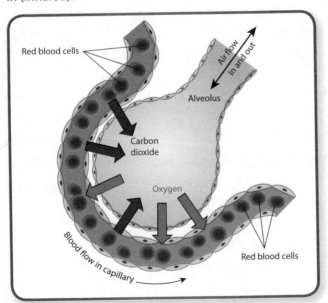

Red blood cells

Air flow In and out

Alveolus

Carbon dioxide

Oxygen

Red blood cells

Blood flow in capillary

The carbon dioxide is not used in animals, so it needs to be removed. It is expelled from the body via the lungs, moving from an area of high CO_2 concentration in the blood flowing through the capillary surrounding an alveolus to an area of low concentration inside the alveolus.

Respiration takes place in all plant cells, too. Water and carbon dioxide are also produced as products. As in animals, the water can be used for hydrolysis reactions, e.g. the formation of glucose from starch. Unlike in animals, some of the carbon dioxide can also be used in photosynthesis.

Nitrogen Metabolism

Nitrogen is a key element for life. All life on Earth is made from protein. Proteins are polymers of amino acids that have been chemically joined by peptide bonds. Amino acids contain amine ($-NH_2$) groups. When excess amino acids are broken down in the liver, the amine groups are converted into ammonium ions (NH_4^+) in a process called **deamination**.

$$2NH_2CHRCOOH + O_2 \; \rightarrow \; 2CROCOOH \; + \; 2NH_3$$

Amino acid oxygen carboxylic acid ammonia

Ammonia is highly toxic. In solution it is in a dynamic equilibrium with ammonium and hydroxide ions.

$$NH_3 \; + \; H_2O \; \rightleftharpoons \; NH_4^+ \; + \; OH^-$$

Ammonia water ammonium ion hydroxyl ion

Enzymes in the liver catalyse the conversion of ammonia to the less toxic urea, along with water.

$$CO_2 \; + \; 2NH_3 \; \rightarrow \; (NH_2)_2CO \; + \; H_2O$$

Carbon dioxide ammonia urea water

Urea is a small, low toxicity, soluble compound, which means that the excess nitrogenous waste can be removed without harming the organism.

$$H_2N \underset{\text{Urea}}{\overset{\displaystyle O}{\diagup\!\!\diagdown}} NH_2$$

Urea dissolves in water to produce urine.

The complete series of reactions leading to the production of urea is called the **ornithine cycle**.

The Liver

The liver could be thought of as being the second most important organ, after the brain. A human liver carries out over 500 different functions. The heart in comparison only has one function, to pump blood around the body. The liver is also the heaviest internal organ in the body. If the liver fails, then the only solution is a complete liver transplant. Such operations are complex and the new liver is likely to be rejected by the body, so survival is low. The majority of the liver functions are to do with breaking down and detoxifying chemicals, such as amino acids. The liver also stores excess glucose as glycogen.

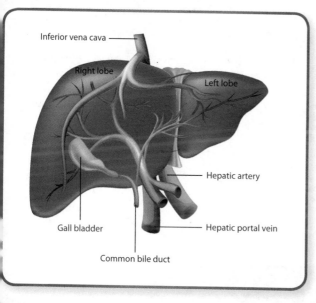

The liver is situated on the right side of the body and is protected by the ribs. The liver has two large sections, the left and right lobes. The liver sits on top of the gall bladder and parts of the pancreas and small intestines.

Blood enters the liver from the **hepatic artery** which brings oxygenated blood from the aorta. Blood also enters the liver from the **hepatic portal vein**. The blood travelling in the hepatic portal vein comes from the entire digestive tract, so is rich in freshly digested materials. Having passed through the liver the blood leaves via the inferior vena cava, which leads directly to the right atrium of the heart.

Histology of the Liver

The liver is made up of millions of cells called **hepatocytes**. The hepatocytes are arranged in hexagonal structures called **hepatic lobules**. The hepatic lobules bring blood to the hepatocytes from arterioles and the hepatic portal vein, In addition, the bile duct also runs through sections of the hepatic lobule.

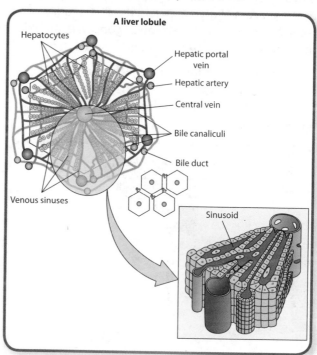

A liver lobule

The blood, rich in dissolved nutrients, passes from the outer edge of the hepatic lobule to the centre, where it leaves the liver.

Sections of the liver can be analysed to identify features, such as in the micrograph below.

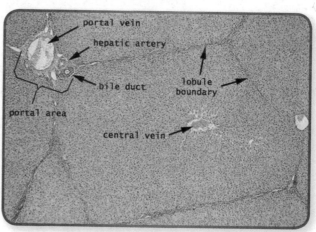

Glycogen

As well as detoxifying toxic chemicals, the liver also stores excess sugar, in the form of glucose. The glucose that enters the blood during digestion first enters the liver via the hepatic portal vein, having passed through the lining of the intestine. The glucose is hydrolysed into the storage polymer glycogen by the process of **glycogenesis**. It can be readily reconverted into glucose by **glycogenolysis** should there be a metabolic requirement.

Glucose can also be formed by **gluconeogenesis** under certain situations. This is where glucose is made using non-carbohydrate molecules, such as glycerol and amino acids.

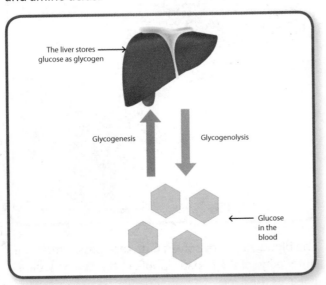

The liver stores glucose as glycogen

Glycogenesis

Glycogenolysis

Glucose in the blood

QUICK TEST

1. How do waste products differ from non-waste products?

2. What is the difference between egestion and excretion?

3. What is the formula for aerobic respiration?

4. True or false? Photosynthesising cells do not respire.

5. What type of monomer is used to form a protein?

6. What are the products of the breakdown of amino acids?

7. What is urea formed from?

8. What two blood vessels transport blood into the liver?

9. What cells make up the majority of the liver?

10. In what form is glucose stored in the liver?

SUMMARY

- Not all products from a metabolic reaction are useful.
- Waste products are those that cannot be used or stored safely.
- Excretion is the removal of waste from an organism.
- Egestion is the removal of non-digested material from a cell or organism.
- Respiration is the liberation of energy from food.
- Aerobic respiration:

$$C_6H_{12}O_6 \ + \ 6O_2 \ \rightarrow \ 6H_2O \ + \ 6CO_2$$

Glucose   oxygen   water   carbon dioxide

- Water produced from respiration can be used in other metabolic reactions.
- The carbon dioxide cannot be used by animals, so is exhaled from the lungs.

- All plant cells also carry out respiration. Some of the carbon dioxide can be used in photosynthesis.

- Nitrogen is a vital element in living organisms. It is present in all amino acids that make proteins, polymers of amino acids joined by peptide bonds.

- Excess amino acids are broken down in the liver to form carboxylic acids and ammonia.

$$2NH_2CHRCOOH \quad + \quad O_2 \quad \rightarrow \quad 2CROCOOH \quad + \quad 2NH_3$$

| Amino acid | oxygen | carboxylic acid | ammonia |

- Ammonia is converted to ammonium ions:

$$NH_3 \quad + \quad H_2O \quad \rightleftharpoons \quad NH_4^+ \quad + \quad OH^-$$

| Ammonia | water | ammonium ion | hydroxyl ion |

- Enzymes catalyse the breakdown of toxic ammonium ions into the less toxic urea.

$$CO_2 \quad + \quad 2NH_3 \quad \rightarrow \quad (NH_2)_2CO \quad + \quad H_2O$$

| Carbon dioxide | ammonia | urea | water |

- Urea dissolves easily in water to make urine.

- The liver is the body's second most important organ, carrying out over 500 functions.

- The liver takes blood from the hepatic artery and hepatic portal vein (from the digestive tract).

- The liver is made up of millions of cells called hepatocytes, arranged in hexagonal structures called hepatic lobules.

- Toxic chemicals are broken down by the hepatocytes.

- Excess sugar is stored in the liver as glycogen and converted back to glucose through glycogenolysis when required.

- Glucose can also be manufactured from non-carbohydrate molecules such as glycerol and amino acids.

- This process is called gluconeogenesis.

PRACTICE QUESTIONS

1. The liver is the second most important organ in the body. One of the functions of the liver is to break down and detoxify chemicals.

   a) i) Through which blood vessels does blood arrive at the liver? [2 marks]

   ii) Which blood vessel transports blood away from the liver? [1 mark]

   b) The liver is made up of a large number of hepatocytes arranged in structures called hepatic lobules. Draw the basic structure of a single hepatic lobule, labelling the key parts. [6 marks]

   c) One function of the liver is to break down ammonia into the less toxic urea. Write the symbol equation for this reaction. [2 marks]

The Kidney

The kidneys are two bean-shaped organs that have a major role in the control of water potential in the blood as well as excretion of the waste products of metabolism. Kidneys are found in reptiles, birds and mammals. They are paired so that, should a kidney fail, there is a backup.

Urinary System

The kidneys are located below the ribs towards the back of the animal.

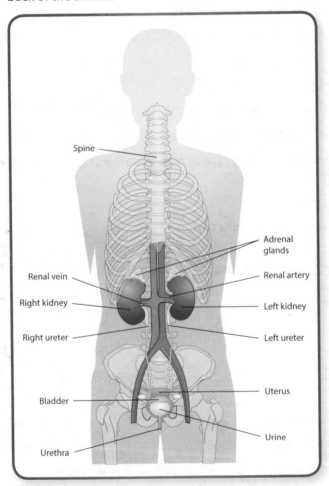

Spine
Adrenal glands
Renal vein
Renal artery
Right kidney
Left kidney
Right ureter
Left ureter
Uterus
Bladder
Urine
Urethra

Each kidney receives blood from a renal artery. Blood leaves each kidney via the renal vein. Urine is transported to the bladder via the ureter. It is stored in the bladder until it is ready to be removed from the body. It then travels through the urethra.

Kidney Structure

The kidney is an organ that is divided into different sections according to the role they carry out.

Surrounding the kidney is a tough layer of connective tissue called the renal fascia. Beneath the fascia, the outermost section of the kidney is called the **renal cortex**. The **renal medulla** is the innermost section of the kidney. It is arranged into pyramid-like sections called **renal pyramids**, which have blood vessels passing through them. The **renal pelvis** acts as a funnel to direct the newly formed urine into the ureter.

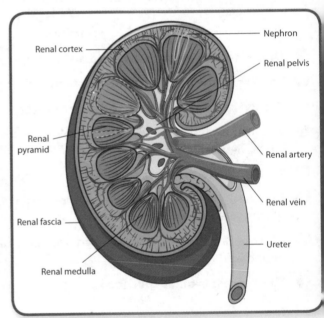

Nephron
Renal cortex
Renal pelvis
Renal pyramid
Renal artery
Renal vein
Renal fascia
Ureter
Renal medulla

The Nephron

The renal cortex and renal medulla are made up of nephrons, the functional unit of the kidney. The nephron is a tube along the length of which blood is filtered and key molecules are removed to form urine. In addition, water and other molecules are reabsorbed when needed. The renal medulla contains the proximal convoluted tubule and the renal corpuscle, comprising **Bowman's capsule** and the **glomerulus**.

The loop of Henle is located in the renal medulla. The loop of Henle's function is to create a concentration gradient in the renal medulla. It is the portion of the nephron that leads from the proximal convoluted tubule to the distal convoluted tubule.

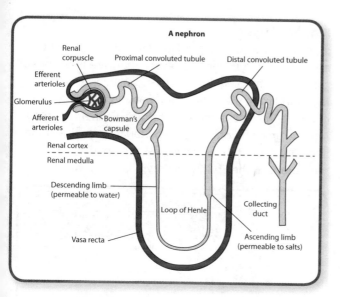

A nephron

- Renal corpuscle
- Proximal convoluted tubule
- Distal convoluted tubule
- Efferent arterioles
- Glomerulus
- Afferent arterioles
- Bowman's capsule
- Renal cortex
- Renal medulla
- Descending limb (permeable to water)
- Loop of Henle
- Collecting duct
- Vasa recta
- Ascending limb (permeable to salts)

Ultrafiltration

The blood enters the glomerulus (a capillary bed) from the afferent arteriole. The glomerulus is housed inside Bowman's capsule. It is here that blood is filtered to remove waste substances. Large proteins and cells remain in the blood, but the waste materials and excess fluid pass through into the nephron. This occurs due to the high pressure of the blood passing through the afferent arteriole. The pressure comes from the afferent arteriole being wider than the efferent arteriole. The blood leaves the glomerulus via the efferent arteriole and then the blood vessel, now called the vasa recta, follows the renal tubule that makes up the rest of the nephron.

Proximal Convoluted Tubule

The proximal convoluted tubule contains cells with **brush borders** to increase surface area. The role of the proximal convoluted tubule is to regulate the pH of the filtrate by exchanging hydrogen ions for bicarbonate ions and reabsorbing glucose and amino acids (**selective reabsorption**). Sodium is also removed from the filtrate and transported back into the blood in the vasa recta.

Loop of Henle

The loop of Henle is a U-shaped structure in the renal medulla. There are four parts of the loop of Henle:

1. Thin descending limb: this has low permeability to ions and urea and high permeability to water.
2. Thin ascending limb: this is not permeable to water but is permeable to ions.

3. Thick ascending limb: sodium, potassium and chloride ions are reabsorbed by active transport using co-transporter proteins. Electrical and concentration gradients cause more reabsorption of sodium ions as well as that of magnesium and calcium.

4. Cortical ascending limb: this is in the renal cortex and drains the urine into the distal convoluted tubule.

The filtration system in the nephron uses **counter-current flow** to ensure that there is always a concentration gradient.

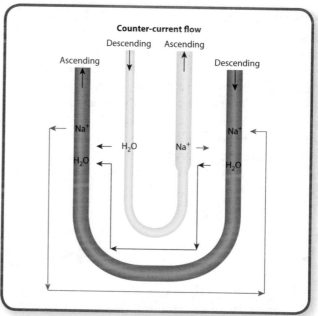

Counter-current flow

Ascending — Descending — Ascending — Descending

Na^+ — H_2O — Na^+ — Na^+
H_2O — Na^+ — H_2O

The blood moves in the opposite direction to the flow of the filtrate. This ensures that there is always a concentration gradient.

Control of Water Potential

The reabsorption of water in the nephron is controlled by **osmoreceptors** in the hypothalamus. These cells expand when the blood plasma is more dilute and contract when there is high concentration in the plasma. The hypothalamus responds by sending a message to the posterior pituitary gland to alter production of antidiuretic hormone (ADH).

ADH is a peptide hormone that increases the permeability of the walls of the collecting ducts and distal convoluted tubule. It does this by opening aquaporin channels that let water pass through, down an osmotic gradient, into the blood. When the blood is too dilute the hypothalamus triggers a reduction in ADH production. This causes water to remain in the filtrate in the nephron. A large volume of dilute urine is made.

When blood is too concentrated the hypothalamus allows more ADH to be released, increasing the permeability of the tubules and leading to water moving from the filtrate back into the blood. A smaller volume of more concentrated urine is produced as a result.

The water potential in the filtrate is higher than the water potential in the blood.

Kidney Failure

If both kidneys fail, then there are two treatments. Donation of a kidney requires either a suitable donor donating one of their working, healthy kidneys or the use of kidneys from a deceased organ donor. The advantage of a live donor is that a person can continue to live with just one functioning kidney. The disadvantage is the greater risks for the donor, through both the surgery to remove the kidney and the future potential for their own, single kidney to fail.

Kidney Dialysis

If an organ transplant is not available then a patient needs to undergo kidney **dialysis**. There are two types of dialysis. Haemodialysis, shown below, involves removing the blood from the patient and passing it through a machine that uses a partially permeable membrane to remove urea and other waste materials from the blood. In contrast, peritoneal dialysis uses the peritoneal membrane in the abdominal cavity to filter the blood.

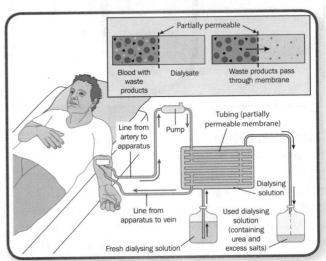

SUMMARY

- The kidneys are involved in controlling water potential in the blood and the excretion of waste products of metabolism. Kidneys are found in reptiles, birds and mammals.

- Each kidney receives blood from a renal artery. The blood exits via the renal veins.

- Urine is transported to the bladder via the ureter. It is stored in the bladder and leaves the body via the urethra.

- The kidney is surrounded by a tough connective tissue called the renal fascia. The outermost section of the kidney is the renal cortex.

- The renal medulla is the innermost section of the kidney, arranged in pyramid-like sections called renal pyramids. Blood vessels pass between the renal pyramids.

- The renal pelvis funnels the newly formed urine into the ureter.

- The renal cortex and renal medulla are made up of nephrons. Blood enters the nephron via the glomerulus (a capillary bed) from the afferent arteriole.

- The glomerulus is contained in the Bowman's capsule and is the location of blood ultrafiltration.

- Large proteins and other molecules remain in the blood whereas waste materials and excess fluid pass through into the nephron, forced by the high pressure.

- The blood leaves the glomerulus via the efferent arteriole into the vasa recta. The vasa recta follows the renal tubule, making up the remainder of the nephron.

- The Bowman's capsule joins to the proximal convoluted tubule which contains cells with brush borders to increase surface area. Here the pH of the filtrate is regulated. This is achieved by exchanging hydrogen ions for bicarbonate ions and reabsorption of glucose and amino acids.
- Sodium ions are removed from the filtrate into the vasa recta.
- The loop of Henle is a U-shaped structure found in the renal medulla. It has four distinct sections.
- The filtration system in the nephron uses a counter-current flow to maintain concentration gradients.
- The hypothalamus controls water balance: sending a signal to the pituitary gland to get it to increase or decrease production of antidiuretic hormone (ADH).
- ADH increases permeability of parts of the nephron, causing water to be reabsorbed. Lack of ADH causes water to remain in the nephron and leave as dilute urine.

QUICK TEST

1. What animals possess kidneys?

2. Give the function of the ureter and urethra.

3. Where does the filtration of blood take place in the nephron?

4. What is the function of the brush borders of the proximal convoluted tubule?

5. What ions are exchanged in the proximal convoluted tubule?

6. Which section of the loop of Henle reabsorbs ions by active transport?

7. How are concentration gradients maximised in the nephron?

8. There is a high level of water in the blood. Describe how the hypothalamus responds.

9. How does ADH affect the nephron?

10. Name a feature of the urine produced in the absence of ADH.

PRACTICE QUESTIONS

1. The diagram below shows a cross section through a human kidney.

   a) Name parts X, Y and Z. **[3 marks]**

   b) What is a nephron and how is it involved in excretion? **[3 marks]**

   c) Describe how the following structures are able to carry out their job:

      i) The glomerulus. **[2 marks]**

      ii) The loop of Henle. **[2 marks]**

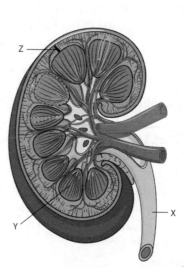

Nervous Communication

Mammals have to coordinate the actions of millions of cells in the body. This coordination is brought about in humans by the nervous system and the endocrine system. The nervous system provides the ability to rapidly coordinate all parts of the body in a very short time interval. The nervous system relies on electrical impulses sent through specially adapted cells, called nerves or **neurones**, at speeds between 1 and 120 m/s.

The nervous system is made up of different parts.

Receptors

The receptors are cells that detect stimuli (changes in the environment). A wide variety of stimuli can be detected by the respective receptor.

- Mechanoreceptors detect pressure changes, e.g. touch.

- Thermoreceptors detect changes in temperature.

- Electromagnetic receptors detect parts of the electromagnetic spectrum, e.g. visible light.

- Nociceptors detect pain from the skin and tissues in the body.

- Chemoreceptors detect the presence or absence of chemicals, such as glucose.

- Proprioceptors detect changes in position, e.g. length or angle.

- Baroreceptors respond to changes in pressure, e.g. in blood vessels.

- Osmoreceptors respond to the changes in water potential, e.g. in the hypothalamus.

Each group can be subdivided into receptors with different roles. The receptor detects a stimulus and then converts it into an electrical impulse. This is called **transduction**.

Effectors

The cells carrying out the response are called the effectors. They may be muscular or they may be **glandular**. The response is sent to the effector in effector neurones (sometimes called motor neurones) via an electrical signal. This is then transduced into a physical response.

Nervous System

The receptors and effectors are part of a nervous system. The central nervous system (CNS) consists of the brain and spinal cord. The peripheral nervous system (PNS) consists of all the nerves other than those in the CNS.

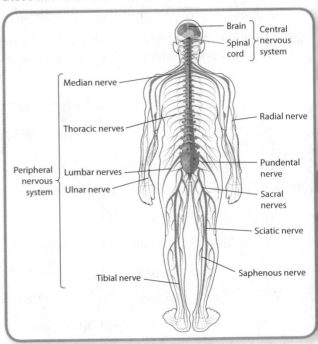

Pacinian Corpuscles

There are four types of mechanoreceptor. One example in the skin are the mechanoreceptors called **Pacinian corpuscles**, which detect vibration and pressure (see figure at the top of the next page).

The Pacinian corpuscle senses stimuli through deformation of the layers making up the capsule. For example, a person picks up a book. This causes the nerve fibre in the centre to bend or stretch. This causes the generation of an **action potential**. (Action potentials are discussed in the next section.) An electrical impulse is sent along the sensory neurone to the brain. A response is then sent to the effector muscle to carry out the response, e.g. to reduce the squeezing of the hand.

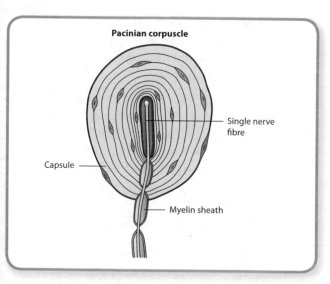

Pacinian corpuscle

Single nerve fibre

Capsule

Myelin sheath

Structure of Neurones

The receptor and effector neurones have certain key features.

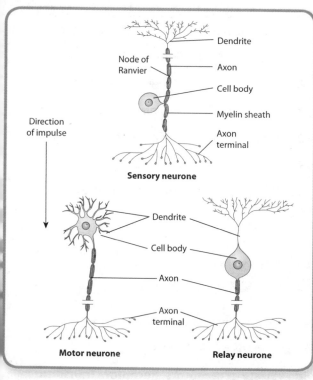

Dendrite

Node of Ranvier

Axon

Cell body

Direction of impulse

Myelin sheath

Axon terminal

Sensory neurone

Dendrite

Cell body

Axon

Axon terminal

Motor neurone

Relay neurone

Dendrites carry electrical signals *to* the cell body. Axons take the signal *away* from the cell body to terminals. At the terminals the electrical signal is converted into a chemical signal to cross the gap (synapse) between the axon terminal and the dendrite of another neurone. The axon is insulated with a myelin sheath.

Sensory neurones detect a stimulus and then pass the signal on to the CNS or a relay neurone.

A relay neurone passes an electrical impulse between neurones.

Motor neurones (or effector neurones) send signals from the cell body, along the axon to the axon terminals. Motor neurones connect to an effector, e.g. a muscle or a gland.

Myelination

The **myelin sheath** is the extended plasma membrane of a Schwann cell that wraps around the axon repeatedly. It contains high levels of cholesterol.

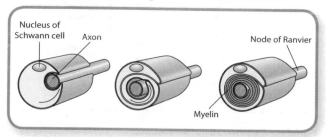

Nucleus of Schwann cell

Axon

Node of Ranvier

Myelin

The myelin sheath has regular gaps, every 1–3 mm, called **nodes of Ranvier**. The gaps are around 2–3 μm wide.

The function of the sheath is to insulate the nerve, preventing crosstalk. The other function of myelin is to speed up the electrical impulse. Neurones with a myelin sheath transmit messages faster than those without. Damage to the myelin sheath causes neuromuscular diseases such as multiple sclerosis.

Some receptors are unmyelinated, including many sensory receptors such as nociceptors, and temperature, touch and certain pressure receptors. These are receptors in the peripheral nervous system and are unmyelinated because speed of impulse is not important.

Proprioceptors and pressure receptors in the skin are always myelinated. Proprioceptors detect changes in angle and length of cells such as muscle. The pressure receptors in the skin, such as the Pacinian corpuscles, detect changes when objects are picked up or squeezed. To coordinate so many muscles the responses have to be dealt with rapidly, so myelination is necessary.

Light Detection

The retina in the human eye contains electromagnetic receptors (photoreceptors) that detect visible light.

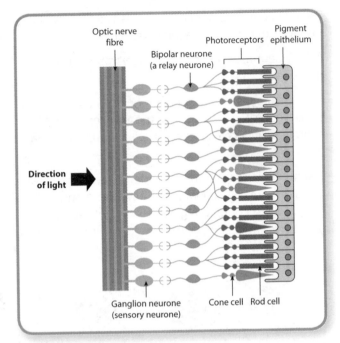

Optic nerve fibre
Photoreceptors
Pigment epithelium
Bipolar neurone (a relay neurone)
Direction of light
Ganglion neurone (sensory neurone)
Cone cell Rod cell

Light passes through the retina and is detected by two types of photoreceptor. Most photoreceptors (around 120 million) are **rod cells**. They are monochromatic, detecting light and dark. They allow vision in low light and detection of movement. There are fewer **cone cells** (around 6 million). They are concentrated in the middle of the retina (the **fovea**) and detect colour and detail. This is why colour is harder to see at night and why humans notice movement in the peripheral vision so easily.

Rods use the pigment **rhodopsin** to detect light. Rhodopsin is extremely sensitive to light and changes shape to form activated rhodopsin. This change

causes a neurotransmitter to pass from a **bipolar neurone** to a sensory neurone, triggering an action potential in the **ganglion neurone**. This sends an electrical impulse to the brain.

A similar process occurs in the cone cells, which contain photosensitive colour pigments (red, green and blue) that trigger an action potential at particular light wavelengths. The brain interprets the signals from each receptor and creates the image.

QUICK TEST

1. Give the speed range for electrical impulses.

2. What are the two parts of the nervous system?

3. What do mechanoreceptors, nociceptors and proprioceptors detect?

4. Other than the receptors given in question 3, give the names of three more receptors.

5. What is transduction?

6. What are the two types of effector?

7. Draw and label a Pacinian corpuscle.

8. What are the three types of neurone?

9. What are nodes of Ranvier?

10. What happens to rhodopsin in the presence of light?

SUMMARY

- The nervous system enables coordination of all parts of the body in a very short period of time.

- Electrical impulses sent through neurones can travel at speeds of 1–120 m/s.

- Receptors are cells that detect stimuli. There is a wide variety of receptors. Receptors transduce the stimulus into an electrical impulse.

- Effectors are cells that carry out the response to a stimulus; they can be muscular or glandular. Electrical impulses from effector neurones are transduced into a physical response.

- The nervous system is categorised as the central nervous system (CNS; brain and spinal cord) and the peripheral nervous system (PNS; all other nerves).

- There are four types of mechanoreceptor.

- Skin mechanoreceptors have Pacinian corpuscles, which deform in response to vibration and pressure.

- There are three types of neurone:
  - sensory, transporting signals from receptor cells
  - relay, passing electrical impulses between neurones
  - effector or motor, sending electrical impulses to the muscle or gland carrying out the response.

- Dendrites carry electrical signals to the cell body of the neurone.

- Axons take the signals away from the cell body.

- A synapse is the gap between an axon terminal and the dendrite of another neurone.

- Axons are insulated with a myelin sheath, with gaps called nodes of Ranvier every 1–3 mm.

- The retina contains rod and cone photoreceptors.

- Rod cells detect light/dark and movement.

- When light hits the pigment rhodopsin it forms activated rhodopsin. This then sends an electrical impulse to the brain.

- Cone cells contain different photoreceptive colour pigments (red, green and blue).

PRACTICE QUESTIONS

1. Look at this diagram of a Pacinian corpuscle.

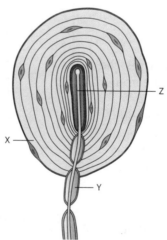

a) Name parts X, Y and Z. [3 marks]

b) What type of receptor is a Pacinian corpuscle? [1 mark]

c) Explain the role of Y. [3 marks]

Electrical Signals

Neurones are structurally similar to electrical wires. Like electrical wires, neurones transmit electrical signals. They are also insulated, to prevent crosstalk (messages in separate neurones being mixed up). Electrical wires are insulated with plastic coating, but in neurones the myelin sheath provides the insulation. The process of sending a nerve impulse is more complex than passing current through a wire, however. The signal that travels through a copper wire is an electrical current. In a neurone the impulse is a short reversal in electrical **potential difference** of the axon's cell surface membrane. This reversal takes place very quickly and passes along the neurone.

Resting Potential

There is an electrical potential difference between the inside of the axon and the environment outside. This is caused by differences in the concentrations of ions inside and outside the axon. A voltage is the difference in electrical potential between two points. The **resting potential** is the potential difference across the neurone's cell surface membrane when it is not being stimulated. Typically it is around −70 mV. This means that the inside of the neurone is 70 mV less than the outside, so the inside is more negative.

Potassium ions easily move through the plasma membrane down a concentration gradient. At rest the potassium ions move from the inside of the neurone to the outside through protein channels that are open all the time. Sodium ions cannot pass through as easily. Although sodium channels are also open all the time, there are fewer of them. Protein molecules inside the neurone cannot move at all, and these have a negative charge.

The only way sodium can leave the neurone is through the action of a **sodium-potassium pump**, which exchanges three sodium ions out for every two potassium ions pumped in. This pump moves ions *against* their concentration gradient. It therefore needs energy to work, in the form of ATP.

The cause of the electrical potential difference is therefore the relative concentrations of sodium ions (Na^+) and potassium ions (K^+) and the presence of negatively charged proteins. During the resting state, there are more sodium ions outside the neurone and more potassium ions inside.

The Action Potential

When a signal is sent along an axon away from the cell body it is called an **action potential**. The first event is a change in the resting potential from −70 mV to 0 mV. This is **depolarisation**. When the depolarisation reaches −55 mV the neurone will trigger an action potential. So, changes to less than −55 mV will not lead to a nerve impulse, only those above −55 mV, which is called the **threshold**. Above −55 mV a nerve impulse will always fire. This is an all-or-nothing response: there is either an impulse or there is not.

The action potential is explained using the diagram on page 22.

The action potential only lasts for a few milliseconds.

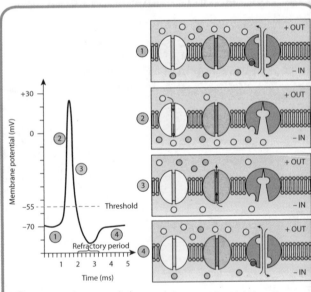

① **Resting potential:** the Na^+/K^+ pump (shown in green, above right) is working, pumping out three Na^+ ions for every two K^+ ions pumped in.

② **Depolarisation:** changes occur to the ion balance, caused by a stimulus. Sodium ions enter through newly opened voltage-gated Na^+ channels (shown as cream-coloured), down their concentration gradient. The inside of the neurone becomes more positive and becomes polarised.

③ **Repolarisation:** voltage-gated K^+ channels open later than the Na^+ channels. The K^+ ions flow out of the neurone down a concentration gradient. The Na^+ channels close. This reverses the depolarisation. The process goes beyond −70 mV (hyperpolarisation) because the K^+ channels (shown in brown) remain open for longer, ensuring that the action potential goes in just one direction.

④ **Resting potential:** finally, the K^+ channels close and the Na^+/K^+ pump continues to exchange three Na^+ out for every two K^+ ions in.

Movement of the Action Potential

The change in polarity moves along the neurone in the following way:

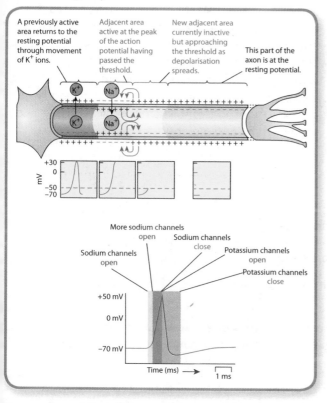

A previously active area returns to the resting potential through movement of K⁺ ions.

Adjacent area active at the peak of the action potential having passed the threshold.

New adjacent area currently inactive but approaching the threshold as depolarisation spreads.

This part of the axon is at the resting potential.

More sodium channels open

Sodium channels close

Potassium channels open

Potassium channels close

Sodium channels open

Frequency of Impulses

After ion channels have opened for the passing action potential there is a resting period before they can open again. This is called the **refractory period**. It allows the proteins of the voltage-sensitive gated channels to return to their original polarity.

The **absolute refractory period** occurs during the action potential and is the time during which another stimulus will not trigger another action potential. This means that there is a maximum frequency of approximately 100 action potentials per second.

Speed of Impulses

Typically nerve impulses can travel between 1 and 120 m/s. Higher temperatures speed up nerve impulses as do axon diameter (the larger the faster) and the presence of a myelin sheath. In myelinated nerves, action potentials are able to jump from one node of Ranvier to the next. This is called saltatory propagation, and allows impulses to travel at 100 m/s rather than 1 m/s.

Synapses

Between the end of an axon and the dendrites of the next axon there is a gap called a synapse. There are two different types of synapse, electrical and chemical. Electrical synapses are very fast and pass messages very quickly and in both directions. They are found only in the heart and the eye. Chemical synapses are slower and require chemicals (called neurotransmitters). They are unidirectional and found throughout the nervous system.

Cholinergic Synapses

Cholinergic synapses are a type of chemical synapse connecting effector neurones with an effector, such as a muscle. The neurotransmitter is **acetylcholine**.

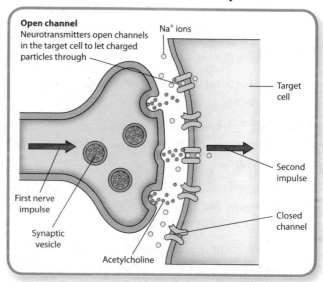

Open channel
Neurotransmitters open channels in the target cell to let charged particles through

Na⁺ ions

Target cell

Second impulse

Closed channel

First nerve impulse

Synaptic vesicle

Acetylcholine

When an action potential reaches the presynaptic membrane at the end of an axon, it triggers the release of acetylcholine, which is held in synaptic vesicles in the presynaptic cytoplasm. The acetylcholine crosses the synapse and attaches to special channel proteins. When the acetylcholine is attached it changes the shape of the channel protein, allowing sodium ions to pass through. The accumulating sodium ions cause depolarisation and trigger an action potential once the electrical potential difference exceeds a particular value in the next axon, and the process continues. Acetylcholine is then broken down by acetylcholinesterase, which is bound to the postsynaptic membrane, into acetate and choline so that the signal does not continue indefinitely. Certain drugs, such as nicotine, can mimic the effects of acetylcholine. Cobra venom can block the receptors, which leads to paralysis and death. Lidocaine blocks voltage-gated Na⁺ ion channels, stopping nerve signals.

Why Chemical Synapses?

Chemical synapses enable the action potential to move in one direction. The process of initiating a new action potential in the next axon is called **summation**. With cholinergic synapses there is spatial summation as there is a physical distance between the neurones. This means that there are less likely to be problems with background noise or interference. Summation allows the signal to be filtered.

Acetylcholine can also trigger action potentials in other axons, so one action potential can trigger action potentials in multiple axons, increasing the dispersion of a nerve signal.

Non-channel Synapses

Unlike cholinergic synapses, non-channel synapses have neuroreceptors that are membrane-bound enzymes rather than channels. When activated by the neurotransmitter, e.g. noradrenaline and adrenaline, they catalyse the production of messenger chemicals that then affect the cell's metabolism. This can include altering the number and sensitivity of ion receptors in the cell. These synapses are involved in long-lasting and slower responses than cholinergic synapses, such as in learning and memory.

SUMMARY

- Myelination insulates the neurone, preventing crosstalk.

- An electrical potential difference is caused by differences in the number of ions inside and outside the axon.

- The resting potential is the potential difference across the neurone membrane when it is not stimulated. The typical value for the resting potential is −70 mV compared to the outside of the axon.

- At rest K^+ ions move easily from the inside of the neurone to the outside down a concentration gradient. Na^+ ions cannot pass through the cell surface membrane as easily. Protein molecules with a negative charge inside the neurone cannot cross the membrane at all.

- The sodium-potassium pump exchanges three Na^+ ions out of the axon for every two K^+ ions into the axon. This causes a build up of K^+ ions and negatively charged proteins inside the neurone and of Na^+ ions outside the neurone at rest.

- The action potential is the movement along the axon of a depolarised region of membrane, initiated at the cell body.

- The first event is a change in resting potential from −70 mV to 0 mV. A stimulus causes Na^+ ions to pass through voltage-gated Na^+ channels. This increases the positive charges in the axon.

- The threshold for an action potential is −55 mV.

- The inside of the neurone is polarised. Voltage-gated K^+ channels then open, allowing K^+ ions to flow out of the neurone down a concentration gradient. Na^+ channels close and the depolarisation is reversed.

- Repolarisation goes beyond −70 mV as the K^+ channels remain open for longer.

- The K^+ channels close and the sodium-potassium pump continues to exchange three Na^+ for every two K^+ ions.

- Overall, the action potential only lasts a few milliseconds.

- The refractory period is the interval before the ion channels can open again. This enables the voltage-gated channels to revert to their original polarity. The refractory period ensures that there is a delay before a stimulus can retrigger an action potential.

- Saltatory propagation is where action potentials can jump (in myelinated neurones) from node to node, thus reaching much faster speeds.

- Synapses are mainly chemical, although electrical synapses exist in the heart and eye. Chemical synapses are unidirectional and require neurotransmitter molecules to pass across the synapse.

- Acetylcholine is released from synaptic vesicles and passes across the synapse to reach channel proteins. The channel proteins allow sodium ions into the neurone, stimulating a new action potential: this is summation.

- Certain drugs, such as nicotine, cobra venom and lidocaine, can interfere with acetylcholine action.

- Summation removes issues with background noise and enables action potentials to be triggered in more than one neurone at the same time.

QUICK TEST

1. What is the cause of the potential difference in a neurone?

2. What is the voltage of the resting potential?

3. What voltage is the threshold for an action potential?

4. Give the ratio of ions passed through the neurone membrane by the sodium-potassium pump.

5. What causes sodium ions to move into the neurone?

6. Why does the depolarisation reverse during an action potential?

7. Why does the potential difference drop to below −70 mV after an action potential?

8. What is the refractory period?

9. Name the neurotransmitter for a cholinergic synapse.

10. What is the approximate maximum rate of action potentials occurring in a myelinated neurone?

PRACTICE QUESTIONS

1. Acetylcholine is a neurotransmitter released into cholinergic synapses. It is then broken down by an enzyme on the postsynaptic membrane.

   a) Acetylcholine diffuses across the synaptic gap and binds onto a receptor on the postsynaptic membrane. Describe how this causes depolarisation of the postsynaptic membrane. **[3 marks]**

   b) Explain why it is important that neurotransmitter is removed from the synapse. **[2 marks]**

   c) Sarin gas is a neurotoxin that binds to acetylcholinesterase. Explain what effect this would have on the diaphragm of a person who had breathed in the gas. **[4 marks]**

Endocrine System

Signals can also be sent through the circulatory system. Chemicals called hormones are secreted from glands directly into the blood. They then travel in the blood to reach specific target cells or tissues in the body. Hormones can regulate an animal's physiology as well as its behaviour. The system of hormonal signalling is called the endocrine system.

Endocrine Glands

Glands in the endocrine system are ductless. They secrete directly into the blood. Glands that have ducts are called exocrine glands, e.g. salivary glands, which secrete saliva. There are a number of major endocrine glands in the human body.

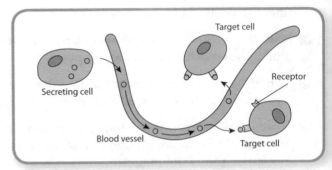

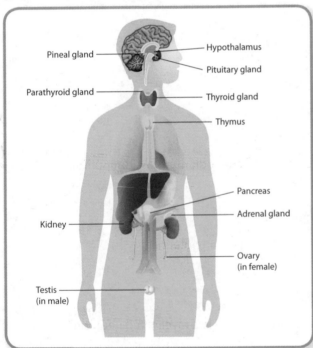

How Signals Are Sent and Received

The hormones are secreted by a gland into the bloodstream. The blood transports the hormone throughout the body, so all cells potentially come into contact with the hormone. Only those with the matching receptor will bind to the hormone and trigger the response, which may be physiological or metabolic.

Adrenal Glands

The adrenal glands are located at the top of the kidneys. They are endocrine glands that produce a variety of hormones, including adrenaline and the steroids aldosterone and cortisol.

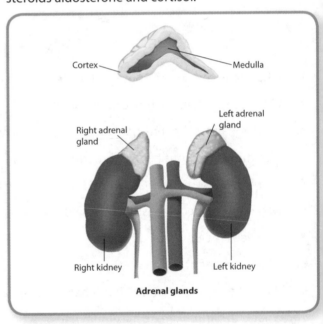

Adrenal glands

The adrenal gland has an adrenal cortex, which is where hormones that are essential and vital for life are produced; e.g. cortisol, which helps to regulate metabolism and enable the body to respond to stress, and aldosterone, which helps regulate blood pressure.

The adrenal medulla, which is in the middle of the adrenal gland, produces hormones that are useful but not vital for life. One example is the hormone adrenaline, which helps the body react to stress. One of the roles of adrenaline is to regulate glycogen.

The Pancreas

The pancreas is a long, flattened endocrine gland located on the underside of the liver and behind the stomach. It produces a number of hormones, including insulin, glucagon and pancreatic polypeptides. In addition to being an endocrine gland, the pancreas is also involved in digestion, secreting various digestive molecules, including pancreatic amylase, via a duct into the duodenum.

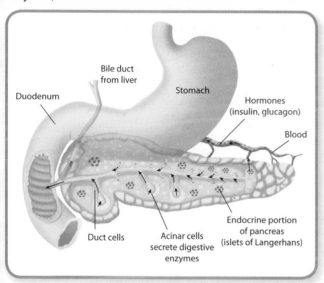

Duodenum

Bile duct from liver

Stomach

Hormones (insulin, glucagon)

Blood

Endocrine portion of pancreas (islets of Langerhans)

Duct cells

Acinar cells secrete digestive enzymes

The islets of Langerhans are the part of the pancreas that produces hormones. The cells that produce digestive enzymes are called acinar cells (or acini).

Looking through a light microscope, the islets of Langerhans are paler than the surrounding acini cells.

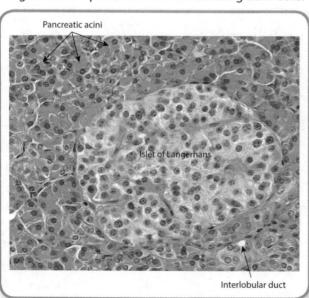

Pancreatic acini

Islet of Langerhans

Interlobular duct

The islets of Langerhans are made up of two types of cell: the alpha cells produce a hormone called glucagon and the beta cells produce the hormone insulin.

QUICK TEST

1. How are signals sent in the endocrine system?

2. Where are the adrenal glands located?

3. Apart from the adrenal glands, name three other endocrine glands.

4. How do endocrine glands differ from exocrine glands, such as the salivary gland?

5. What must be present on a cell for a hormone to be able to act on it?

6. Where in the adrenal gland is adrenaline produced?

7. What hormones are produced in the adrenal cortex?

8. What cells in the pancreas produce digestive enzymes?

9. Give the names of the cells in the islets of Langerhans that produce hormones.

10. What are the two hormones produced by the islets of Langerhans?

- The endocrine system sends signals via hormones. They are secreted by glands into the circulatory system.

- Glands that have ducts are called exocrine glands, such as the salivary glands, which secrete saliva.

- Hormones travel throughout the body and act on specific cells or tissues. They affect physiology as well as behaviour.

- Endocrine glands are ductless glands that secrete hormones directly into the blood.

- They are spread throughout the body and include those shown on the figure.

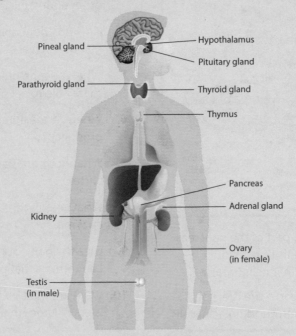

- Receptors specific to a particular hormone are found on the cell surface membrane of target cells.

- The adrenal glands produce a variety of hormones. The adrenal cortex produces hormones essential to life, such as the steroids aldosterone and cortisol. The adrenal medulla produces hormones not essential to survival, such as adrenaline.

- The pancreas produces hormones such as insulin, glucagon and pancreatic polypeptides. It also produces digestive enzymes to help digestion.

- The islets of Langerhans in the pancreas produce hormones and are surrounded by acinar cells that produce the digestive enzymes. The islets of Langerhans have two types of cell. Alpha cells produce the hormone glucagon and beta cells produce the hormone insulin.

PRACTICE QUESTIONS

1. The diagram below shows the endocrine system in a human.

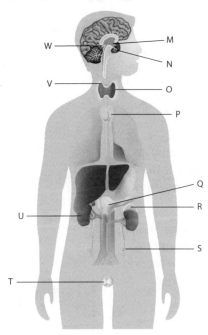

a) Match the descriptions for each gland to the correct location in the body:

    i) Produces the steroid hormones aldosterone and cortisol. **[1 mark]**

    ii) Produces glucagon and insulin. **[1 mark]**

b) Describe the endocrine function of the pancreas. **[3 marks]**

c) Look at the image of a section from the pancreas

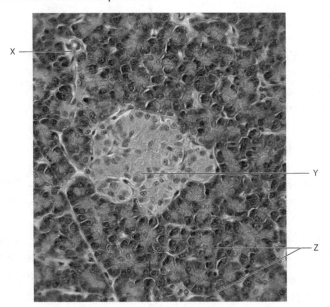

    Name the sections indicated by X, Y and Z. **[3 marks]**

Control of Blood Glucose

Blood Glucose Levels

The monosaccharide glucose is the primary source of energy in the mammalian body. Although glucose is an important molecule, it has to be carefully controlled. If the blood contains too much glucose, then the excess sugar can cause complications, including damage to the kidneys, nerves, cardiovascular system, retina (causing blindness) and the feet and legs. The reason for the damage is these organs absorb glucose directly from the blood; they are open to glucose uptake continuously.

The majority of cells in the body – muscle, liver and fat cells – will only allow glucose in when the hormone **insulin** is present. The reason why these cells respond to insulin is thought to be to protect them when blood glucose levels are high.

Insulin

Insulin is a hormone produced by the **beta cells** of the **islets of Langerhans** in the pancreas. Beta cells respond rapidly to increased glucose concentrations by secreting stored insulin. The beta cells are also stimulated to manufacture more insulin.

Insulin Production

Potassium channels in the cell surface membranes of the beta cells are normally open, whereas voltage-gated calcium channels are normally closed. Potassium ions diffuse out of the beta cells down a concentration gradient. In a similar way to neurones, the inside of the cell becomes negative relative to the outside of the cell, creating a cell surface membrane potential of −70 mV.

If the glucose concentration outside the cell increases then the glucose molecules move into the cell through GLUT2 transporters. The glucose is metabolised to produce ATP. This increases the ratio of ATP to ADP in the cell.

The potassium channels detect the change in ATP levels and close, stopping potassium ions from diffusing out of the cell. This starts to make the cell surface membrane potential more positive. The change in potential difference causes the voltage-gated calcium channels

to open, allowing calcium ions to move into the beta cell, down a concentration gradient. This movement is linked to the movement of insulin, stored in vesicles, out of the cell.

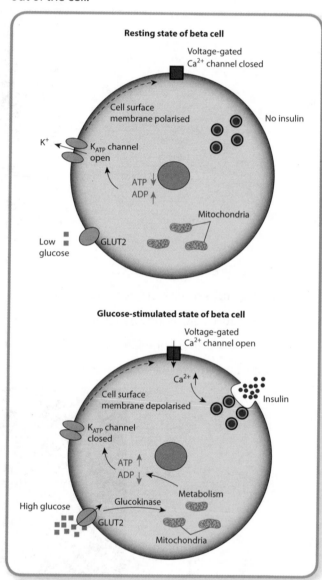

Resting state of beta cell

Glucose-stimulated state of beta cell

Insulin Release

After food is eaten the beta cells are stimulated to release insulin into the blood. The insulin moves through the entire body and binds to receptors on liver, muscle and fat cells.

When insulin is attached to a receptor, an **insulin signalling pathway** is initiated. This enables changes in lipid metabolism, growth and protein metabolism. It also sends a signal for a glucose receptor, GLUT4, to pass glucose into the cell.

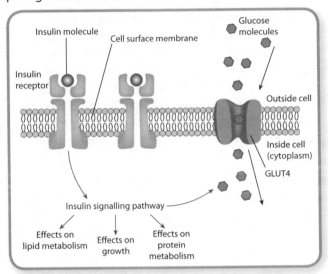

The insulin can be thought of as acting like a key, unlocking the cell and allowing glucose to move in.

The insulin also affects the liver. If there is too much glucose in the blood then the liver will convert the glucose into the storage molecule glycogen.

Glucagon

Glucagon is produced by the **alpha cells** in the islets of Langerhans in the pancreas. Glucagon is a counterbalance to insulin. When blood glucose levels in the blood drop, glucagon is produced, supressing insulin release. The hormone adrenaline also attaches to muscle cells, activating enzymes involved in the conversion of glycogen to glucose. This ensures the rapid release of glucose. The glucagon is transported to the liver and muscles, triggering the cells to break down glycogen into glucose. Glucagon also works in gluconeogenesis where glucose is produced from non-carbohydrates such as glycerol and amino acids. This prevents blood sugar levels from dropping further and prepares the animal for fight or flight.

The actions of insulin and glucagon are both examples of negative feedback. Together, the hormones prevent blood glucose levels from getting too high (**hyperglycaemia**) or too low (**hypoglycaemia**). This relationship can be summarised in the following diagram.

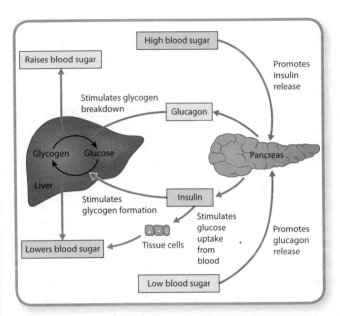

Diabetes

Diabetes mellitus is a condition in which blood glucose levels cannot be controlled. There are three types of diabetes.

Type I

Type I diabetes is a condition resulting from the immune system destroying the beta cells in the pancreas. As a result, the pancreas ceases to produce insulin and the body cannot regulate blood glucose levels. Of all the people suffering from diabetes, approximately 10% will have type I diabetes.

The symptoms are an increased need to urinate, increased thirst and hunger, and weight loss. Typically the condition emerges during childhood.

The cause of type I diabetes can be genetic or environmental. It is theorised that a viral infection can trigger an auto-immune response that destroys the beta cells in the pancreas.

Type II

The vast majority of people with diabetes have type II diabetes. It has the same symptoms as type I diabetes, but the cause differs. With this form of diabetes the islets of Langerhans cells in the pancreas break down. This is due to the muscle, liver and fat cells in the body becoming less sensitive to insulin. This means more insulin has to be produced by the beta cells to have the same effect, putting them under extreme pressure, causing them to fail.

Gestational Diabetes

Sometimes a pregnant woman can't produce the required amount of insulin (two to three times the normal amount) during the pregnancy. This can be because hormones interfere with insulin production or because the growth of the foetus increases the demand for insulin to a level that is too high. Gestational diabetes is temporary and usually disappears after pregnancy.

Treatments

Type I diabetes cannot be prevented, but it can be managed through monitoring blood glucose levels and injecting insulin when needed.

Type II diabetes is prevented by maintaining a healthy body weight. Treatment involves managing diet to ensure it doesn't contain too much glucose. This is normally achieved by reducing the intake of carbohydrates. Drugs can also be prescribed that reduce the amount of glucose in the blood.

If the condition worsens then the patient may need injections of insulin. It is also possible to undergo weight-loss surgery to reduce body mass if the patient cannot lose weight naturally.

Potential Treatments

Insulin used to be produced by extracting it from pigs. This had some issues, one being that people who followed religions banning the use of pigs as a food source could not have the insulin. The advent of genetic engineering led to the production of human insulin in large quantities. The gene for insulin is inserted into a bacterium. The bacteria are grown to large numbers in culture and the insulin is then harvested from the bacteria.

Scientists are now investigating the potential of using stem cells to replace the damaged cells in the pancreas. The stem cells could have the genes coding for beta cells switched on, re-enabling the pancreas to produce insulin.

SUMMARY

- The primary source of energy in mammals is the monosaccharide, glucose.
- Too much glucose in the blood can cause kidney, nerve and cardiovascular damage as well as blindness.
- Liver, muscle cells and fat cells are the *only* cells to allow glucose to enter in the presence of the hormone insulin. This is thought to ensure that these cells are protected if glucose levels are high.
- Insulin is produced by beta cells in the islets of Langerhans of the pancreas when glucose levels increase.
- Like nerve cells, control of insulin is through a membrane potential. K^+ channels are normally open whereas voltage-gated Ca^{2+} channels are closed. K^+ ions diffuse out of the beta cells down a concentration gradient.
- The inside of the cell becomes negative to the outside, creating a membrane potential of -70 mV.
- When glucose levels increase, the molecules move through GLUT2 transporters. The glucose is metabolised to produce ATP, increasing the ratio of ATP to ADP. The K^+ channels detect the change and close.
- The inside of the cell becomes more positive. This causes the voltage-gated Ca^{2+} channels to open, allowing Ca^{2+} into the cell.
- The movement of Ca^{2+} ions is linked to vesicles releasing insulin from the cell.
- The released insulin moves through the entire body and binds to receptors on muscle, liver and fat cells.
- When insulin is attached to its receptor an insulin signalling pathway is initiated. This leads to changes in lipid metabolism, growth and protein metabolism.

- The glucose receptor, GLUT4, then allows glucose to pass into the cell. If there is too much glucose in the blood, the liver converts it into the storage molecule glycogen.
- Glucagon is the counterbalance to insulin. When glucagon is produced (when glucose levels drop) it suppresses insulin.
- The glucagon is transported to the liver and muscles, triggering the breakdown of glycogen into glucose. This prevents blood sugar levels from getting too low.
- Insulin and glucagon together prevent blood glucose levels getting too high (hyperglycaemia) or too low (hypoglycaemia).
- Diabetes mellitus is a condition where blood sugar levels cannot be controlled. Type I diabetes is where the immune system destroys the beta cells so no insulin is produced. Type II diabetes is where the islets of Langerhans break down, as the liver, muscle and fat cells become less sensitive to insulin. More insulin has to be produced by the beta cells to have the same effect, and the pressure causes failure.
- Type I diabetes is managed through monitoring blood glucose and injecting insulin whereas type II is managed by altering the diet, taking exercise and with medicinal drugs. Gestational diabetes (which is distinct from diabetes mellitus), which occurs during pregnancy when the foetus makes demands on the mother to produce more insulin, is usually temporary.
- In the future stem cells could be used to replace the damaged cells in the pancreas.

QUICK TEST

1. Suggest why too much glucose in the blood is dangerous in the long term.
2. Which cells need insulin to allow glucose to enter?
3. What does it mean if a person is hypoglycaemic?
4. What two ions are involved in the release of insulin?
5. What channel protein allows glucose into the beta cell?
6. What is the name of the receptor unlocked by insulin?
7. What is the role of glucagon?
8. How does type II diabetes differ from type I?
9. How does a sufferer of type II diabetes control their blood sugar levels?
10. Suggest how, in the future, patients may be treated for diabetes.

PRACTICE QUESTIONS

1. Over 3.9 million people in the UK are known to have diabetes and this is expected to rise to 5 million people by 2025. It is also estimated that a further 590 000 people have the condition but are unaware of it. The World Health Organization states that it will be the seventh leading cause of death by 2030.

   a) Explain how type I diabetes is caused. [2 marks]

   b) Describe how blood sugar is controlled by insulin and glucagon. [6 marks]

   c) Suggest why 590 000 people in the UK may have diabetes but not be aware that they have the condition. [3 marks]

Plant Growth Regulators

Like animals, plants can respond to stimuli. The responses are to **abiotic** and **biotic** factors (or stresses). Abiotic factors are non-living whereas biotic factors are due to the actions of other organisms.

Abiotic Stress

Abiotic factors have the biggest impact on the growth of plants. There are many types of abiotic stress: lack of light, high and low temperatures, high wind speed, drought, flood and wildfire are all common examples.

The response to many abiotic factors is growth. This can move the plant away from the stress or manoeuvre it into a more beneficial situation. Growth or movement in response to an environmental stimulus is called a **tropism**.

There are a wide range of tropisms, including:

- phototropism: movement or growth in response to light
- geotropism (gravitropism): movement or growth in response to gravity
- heliotropism: diurnal or seasonal motion of the parts of a plant in the direction of the sun.
- thermotropism: movement or growth in response to temperature
- thigmotropism: movement or growth in response to touch
- chemotropism: movement or growth in response to chemicals.

Biotic Stress

Biotic stresses are those caused by other organisms. In many instances plants produce chemical responses when herbivores eat the plant. The response can be always present in the plant or it can be induced in reaction to damage or stress. For example, the action of chewing a plant part may induce the production of secondary metabolites in the consumed part that can affect the herbivore. This can change the herbivore's behaviour by repelling it, or poisoning it, making further consumption of the plant unlikely.

Tannins

One such chemical defence is the production of tannins. Tannins are accumulated in the vacuoles of plants. They can also be produced in response to a herbivore consuming leaves. Tannins can make the plant material difficult to digest, interfering with protein digestion.

Alkaloids

Derived from amino acids, **alkaloids** are chemicals that have a **pharmacological** effect on animals. They can interfere or inhibit enzyme action, prevent DNA synthesis and repair and affect the nervous system. Examples include:

- nicotine and caffeine (both act as insecticides)
- morphine and cocaine (both drugs)
- strychnine (a metabolic poison).

The alkaloids are also known for having a bitter taste, which puts a herbivore off eating more of the plant.

Pheromones

When damaged, some plants release volatile chemicals called **pheromones**. The pheromones attract the natural predators of the insects consuming the plant, as in the figure below. They are also believed to induce similar defensive responses in nearby plants.

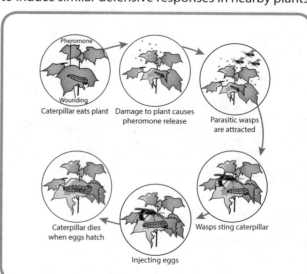

Caterpillar eats plant | Damage to plant causes pheromone release | Parasitic wasps are attracted

Caterpillar dies when eggs hatch | Injecting eggs | Wasps sting caterpillar

Mechanical Responses

Some plants respond mechanically rather than chemically to herbivores. This often involves the leaves folding in response to touch. When the leaves of *Mimosa pudica* (also known as the sensitive plant) are touched, a rapid response ensues. The leaflets fold rapidly and the leaf droops downwards. This is believed to frighten the herbivore and lead it to eat a plant that isn't moving. An alternative theory suggests that the response is to dislodge insects.

Photomorphogenesis

Flowering is controlled by pigments that respond to light. Phytochrome is a blue-green pigment that responds to red wavelengths of light. In the presence of red light of wavelength 660 nm, phytochrome changes conformation to form the active P_{fr} (f_r = far red). When P_{fr} absorbs far-red light of wavelength 730 nm (near infrared) it changes conformation back into P_r (r = red), which is inactive. The ratio of P_{fr} to P_r enables the plant to determine the season and whether to produce flowers, set winter buds or undergo vegetative growth.

Plant Growth Regulators

Plant growth regulators (or plant hormones) are a collection of chemicals that influence the growth and differentiation of plant cells, tissues and organs. Plant growth regulators are involved in all aspects of plant growth and development.

Leaf Loss

Deciduous trees lose their leaves in the autumn. This process is called **abscission** and was thought to involve a plant growth regulator called abscisic acid (ABA) because high levels of ABA were found in leaves that had fallen from trees. The hormone even got its name from this theory.

In recent years, however, it has been determined that the plant growth regulators auxin and ethylene are the primary triggers for leaf drop. Auxin produced in the leaf stops the cells at the site of abscission being sensitive to ethylene. When auxin levels decline in response to changes in day length, ethylene sensitivity of the abscission zone increases. Auxin and ethylene are antagonistic. The rise in ethylene is thought to trigger the activation of cellulase enzymes that break down the cell walls of the cells connected to the leaf, causing the leaf to drop off.

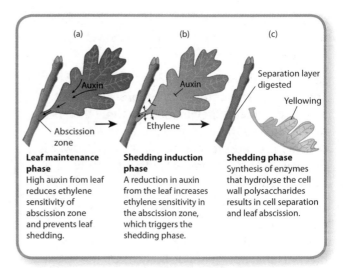

(a)

Leaf maintenance phase
High auxin from leaf reduces ethylene sensitivity of abscission zone and prevents leaf shedding.

(b)

Shedding induction phase
A reduction in auxin from the leaf increases ethylene sensitivity in the abscission zone, which triggers the shedding phase.

(c)

Shedding phase
Synthesis of enzymes that hydrolyse the cell wall polysaccharides results in cell separation and leaf abscission.

Seed Germination

Although ABA is not directly involved in leaf abscission, it is involved in seed germination. The presence of ABA prevents a seed from germinating. This is important as otherwise a seed may start to germinate in the developing fruit. This non-germinating state of the seed is called dormancy. Just before germination ABA levels decrease. When the seedling is growing, ABA levels drop further. When the ABA levels decline another plant growth regulator, **gibberellin**, acts. Gibberellin and ABA are antagonistic to each other. Gibberellins stimulate the expression of enzymes needed for metabolism and growth.

Only when fully functional leaves are produced do ABA levels increase again, slowing growth of the now more mature parts of the plant by inhibiting the action of gibberellins.

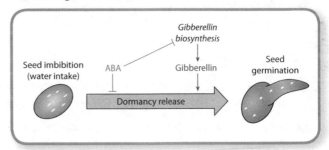

Closure of Stomata

ABA is also involved in the opening and closing of stomata. ABA is produced by cells in the roots in response to a reduction in the water potential of the soil. It travels up the plant to the leaves where it alters the osmotic balance of the stomatal guard cells, causing them to swell and close the stomal opening. Closure of stomata prevents water loss from the leaf.

Apical Dominance

The apex (the tip of the topmost growing shoot) of a plant dominates growth more strongly than the side branches. This is termed apical dominance. Its purpose is to ensure that the plant grows upwards to the light and outcompetes other plants for the same resource.

The main plant growth regulator that causes this effect is auxin. The apical bud produces auxin, which travels down the plant stem in the phloem and prevents the growth of side branches. If the apical bud at the top of a growing shoot is removed, then the reduction in auxin concentration causes the side branches to grow. Eventually one will become dominant and outcompete the other.

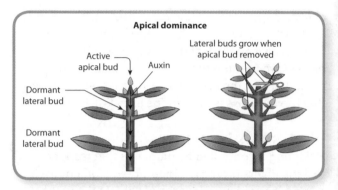

Apical dominance

Active apical bud — Auxin

Lateral buds grow when apical bud removed

Dormant lateral bud

Dormant lateral bud

Stem Elongation

The main plant growth regulator involved in the elongation of plant stems is gibberellin. The presence of gibberellins causes the cells in the stem to elongate. They were first discovered by researchers in Japan who noticed that a fungus, *Gibberella fujikoroi*, caused rice plants to grow extremely tall and then collapse. The fungus was producing the plant growth regulator gibberellin.

SUMMARY

- Plants respond to biotic (living) and abiotic (non-living) factors.

- Abiotic factors have the biggest impact on plant growth. They include lack of light, high and low temperatures, high wind speed, drought, flood and wildfire.

- The response to many abiotic factors is growth of the plant away from the stress or to a more beneficial location.

- Growth in response to an environmental stimulus is called a tropism. There are a wide range of tropisms, including phototropism, geotropism (gravitropism), heliotropism, thermotropism, thigmotropism and chemotropism.

- Biotic stresses are often chemical, e.g. toxins released when a herbivore eats the plant. Chewing induces the production of secondary metabolites that change the herbivore's behaviour. This can include discouraging the animal from eating further or poisoning it.

- Tannins are an example of a chemical defence, making a plant difficult to digest.

- Alkaloids are derived from amino acids and have a pharmacological effect on animals. They can interfere or inhibit enzymes, DNA synthesis and repair and affect the nervous system.

- Pheromones can be produced by plants, attracting the natural predators of the insect consuming the plant.

- Some plants close their leaves to prevent herbivores eating the plants.

- Plant growth regulators (PGRs) are substances that influence plant growth and development.

- Leaf loss is caused by a decrease in auxin, making the abscission site more sensitive to another PGR, ethylene. Ethylene triggers activation of enzymes that break down cell walls at the abscission site. This weakens the leaf and causes it to drop.

- Abscisic acid (ABA) prevents seeds germinating too early, e.g. while still in the fruit. Just before germination ABA levels drop, allowing another PGR, gibberellin, to stimulate growth. ABA and gibberellin are antagonistic to each other.

- ABA is produced by the cells of roots in response to reduced water production in the soil. It travels up to the leaves and alters the osmotic balance of the guard cells, causing them to swell. This closes the stomata, preventing further water loss from the plant.

- The elongation of the plant stem is controlled by PGRs. Gibberellin causes the cells in the stem to elongate.

QUICK TEST

1. What are biotic and abiotic factors?

2. Which has the biggest impact on growth?

3. How does a plant respond with phototropism and chemotropism?

4. Name three plant tropisms other than the two mentioned in question 3.

5. How can a plant's chemicals affect a herbivore that is feeding on it?

6. What are alkaloids derived from?

7. What are PGRs?

8. How are PGRs involved in leaf drop?

9. Describe how PGRs are involved in germination.

10. How does the PGR gibberellin affect plant stems?

PRACTICE QUESTIONS

1. a) Gibberellins are involved in controlling the dormancy of seeds.

   i) What type of compound is gibberellin? **[1 mark]**

   ii) Calculate the rate of growth of the plant hypocotyls between days 3 and 6. Show your working. Give your answer in mm/day to three significant figures. **[2 marks]**

   b) Describe and explain the results of the experiment. **[4 marks]**

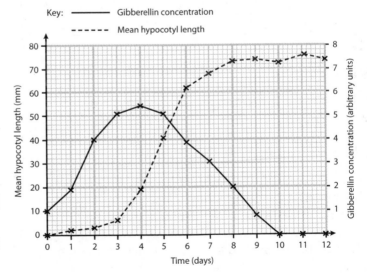

Key: —— Gibberellin concentration

- - - - Mean hypocotyl length

Plant Experiments

Understanding how plants respond to abiotic and biotic factors requires experimental analysis. Unlike with animal experimentation, there are no **ethical issues** to consider when working with plants. In addition, plant experiments are simpler because plants do not move around like animals and are (relatively) easy to grow and reproduce. Experimental observations can alter current theories about how plant growth regulators affect the plant.

Phototropism

The tropic response to light was investigated extensively by Charles Darwin, who published his findings in 1880. On a simple level, experiments can be used to show how plants respond to directional changes in light.

Darwin set up experiments using the **coleoptiles** of canary grass seedlings. Subjecting the coleoptiles to a directional light source led to the coleoptiles growing towards the source. Darwin then removed the apex of the coleoptile. The coleoptiles failed to grow. He then covered the apex, rather than removing it. The coleoptiles also failed to grow towards the light source. Darwin theorised that the apex of the coleoptile was light sensitive, whereas the rest of the shoot was not. Boysen-Jensen did further experiments in the early twentieth century.

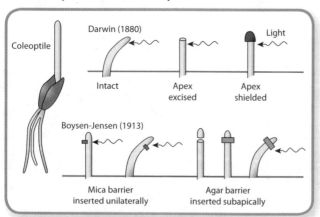

In the early twentieth century, scientists were able to insert a **mica barrier** on either side of the coleoptile. When the barrier was on the same side as the light source the coleoptile grew and bent towards the light source as normal. If the barrier was placed on the opposite side from the light source the coleoptile did not respond to light. This indicated that the chemical must move down the plant on the side away from the light. The substance caused cell growth.

Other scientists, such as Paál in 1919, moved the coleoptile and reset it off centre. This led to the coleoptile continuing to grow as if growing towards a light source, even if it was dark. This supported the hypothesis that a substance was being produced in the tip.

In 1926, Fritz Went, a Dutch scientist, removed the tip of a coleoptile and placed it onto an **agar jelly** block. When the tip was replaced on the coleoptile, the coleoptile grew as normal. If the agar block was placed on the coleoptile, but set to one side, the coleoptile grew more on the side of the agar block, as if it were growing towards a light source. The chemical substance that was in the coleoptile apex must have moved into the agar block.

Went called the substance auxin. After World War II auxin was identified as being **indole-3-acetic acid** (or **IAA**). There are now known to be many different types of auxin.

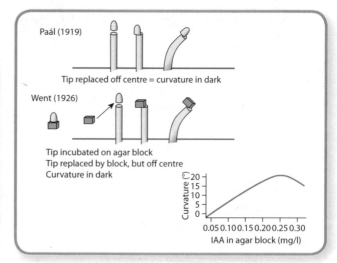

Geotropism

In a similar way to light, geotropism (or gravitropism) has been investigated extensively in the past 200 years.

One experiment involved using a device called a **clinostat**. A clinostat enables seeds to germinate at an angle. Over time the pot containing the seeds can be rotated. This helps to determine the ability of seedlings to respond to a change in the direction of gravity.

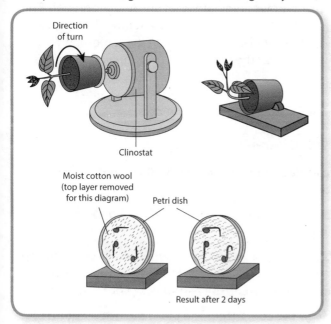

Following experiments with clinostats, scientists were able to carry out experiments similar to those involving removal of coleoptile shoot tips.

With geotropism, the root tip produces auxin. Unlike phototropism, in roots auxin has the opposite effect to that seen in coleoptiles. In roots, the presence of auxin inhibits growth. In contrast, in shoots auxin promotes growth.

Mechanism of Auxin Action

In shoots, the presence of auxin induces cell elongation. Directional light sources cause the auxin to move away from the light. Thus, the cells furthest away from the light source grow more, which causes the shoot to bend towards the light. This is how plants can move in response to the sun tracking across the sky during the day.

We say that plant shoots are positively phototropic, as they move towards light. Roots move away from light, so they are negatively phototropic.

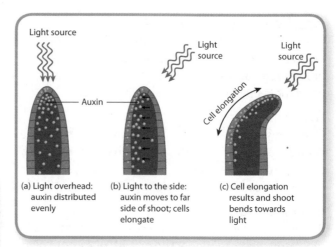

(a) Light overhead: auxin distributed evenly

(b) Light to the side: auxin moves to far side of shoot; cells elongate

(c) Cell elongation results and shoot bends towards light

The opposite applies with gravity. Plant shoots are negatively geotropic: they move away from gravity. Roots are positively geotropic because they grow towards the source of gravity.

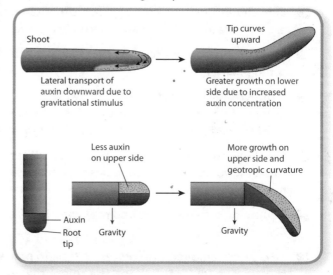

Apical Dominance

Demonstrating apical dominance is relatively simple. The apical meristem (the growing tip) of a shoot can be removed. This then leads to the growth of side branches. If the apical meristem is removed and an agar block containing auxin added, then apical dominance continues.

Stem Elongation

As with apical dominance, experiments can demonstrate the effect of a plant growth regulator on stem elongation. Addition of gibberellin causes stem elongation. If the levels of plant growth regulator are increased then elongation increases.

Application of Understanding

Understanding how plant growth regulators work has led to their commercial use. Scientists can use plant growth regulators to influence the ripening of fruit, grow roots on cuttings and even kill weeds.

Fruit Ripening

Plant growth regulators such as ethylene can be used to control ripening of fruit. This means that supermarkets can sell fruit that are at their peak of ripeness, so that consumers can eat them straight away.

Rooting Powders

Rooting powders contain a mix of plant growth regulators that can trigger the growth of roots in plant cuttings. This means that many clones of a plant can be created, all with the same desired traits. The main plant growth regulator used is auxin.

Weed Killers

Some plant growth regulators can also be used as weedkillers. As plant growth regulators have specific effects on a particular group of plants, these weedkillers are selective. The weedkiller contains a plant growth regulator that encourages growth. They also have analogues of the plant growth regulator that cannot be metabolised in the same way. This means that the plants effectively grow themselves to death.

SUMMARY

- Experiments on tropisms of plants do not involve ethical considerations. Plants do not move around like animals and are relatively easy to grow.

- Phototropisms were researched extensively by Charles Darwin, who used the coleoptiles of canary grass.

- A directional light source caused growth towards the light source but removing the apex led to the failure of the coleoptile to grow. With a covered apex the coleoptile also failed to grow towards the light source, indicating that the apex was light sensitive whereas the rest of the shoot was not.

- Later scientists added a mica barrier on either side of the coleoptile. The plant did not respond to the directional source if the mica was in the side furthest away from the source, showing that there must be a chemical produced by the apex that caused growth.

- Removing the coleoptile and replacing it off centre led to the plant growing as if it were towards a light source.

- Fritz Went removed the coleoptile tip and placed it on a block of agar jelly. When the block was replaced on top of the shoot, the coleoptile grew as if the apex were still there. The chemical must have moved into the agar block. Went called the substance auxin.

- After World War II the auxin was identified as being indole-3-acetic acid (IAA). There are many different types of auxin.

- Geotropism was shown to respond in a similar way to phototropism.

- Experimentation using clinostats showed that the root tip produces auxin. Unlike the auxin in a shoot, it has the opposite effect in a root: inhibiting growth.

- In shoots the presence of auxin causes cell elongation. A directional light source makes the auxin move away from the source. The cells on the side furthest away from the light source grow, due to the presence of auxin. The shoot is positively phototropic.

- In roots, when auxin moves towards the gravitational source, the cells with auxin do not grow, so the root grows down towards the source of gravity.

- Apical dominance is demonstrated by removal of a shoot tip; this encourages side branches to grow.
- Understanding how plant growth regulators work has led to their commercial application.
- Manipulation of fruit ripening, rooting of cuttings and the action of some weedkillers are all possible because of our understanding of plant growth regulators.

QUICK TEST

1. Give three reasons why experimenting on plants is easier than working on animals.

2. Who was the famous scientist who experimented on phototropism in the 1800s?

3. What part of canary grass did he experiment with?

4. Describe how it was proven that the apex produced a chemical that caused growth.

5. What did Fritz Went use to collect the chemical?

6. What is the name of the chemical?

7. What device is used to experiment with geotropism?

8. How do roots respond to the chemical named in question 6?

9. How can apical dominance be shown experimentally?

10. Give three ways that plant growth regulators have been used commercially.

PRACTICE QUESTIONS

1. Broad beans are being grown horizontally.

Broad bean seedlings pinned to damp paper towel and cork base board

a) What tropism is being tested? [1 mark]

b) After a day the root of one of the broad bean seedlings was examined. The roots had bent downwards. Describe how the distribution of indole-3-acetic acid (IAA) caused the roots to bend. [2 marks]

c) Draw a diagram to show the IAA distribution in a shoot being lit by a light source that is positioned on the right. [2 marks]

Nervous System Organisation

The mammalian nervous system is structurally organised into the central nervous system and peripheral nervous system. The nervous system can also be categorised according to its function, in terms of the **somatic** and **autonomic** nervous systems.

Somatic Nervous System

The somatic nervous system is the part of the peripheral nervous system that is associated with voluntary control of the body's movements. This includes movement of muscles and organs as well as reflex actions. The process involves sensory neurones connected to sense organs and receptors sending electrical impulses to the brain and spinal cord, with the response being relayed to the effector neurones.

Autonomic Nervous System

The autonomic nervous system is responsible for the control of all bodily functions that are not under direct conscious control, such as breathing, heart rate, digestion and hormone production.

Brain Anatomy

The brain is the main organ in the mammalian nervous system and the most complex. It is located in the head and protected by thick bones in the skull. The brain has a number of distinct structures that carry out different roles.

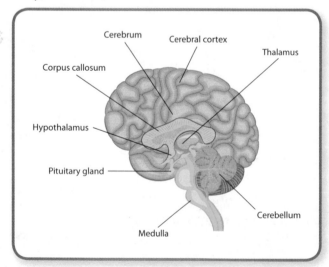

Cerebrum

The brain is divided into two halves, the left and right hemispheres. The outer surface of the brain is the **cerebrum**. This controls perception, voluntary movement and learning. The two hemispheres communicate through a thick band of neurones called the corpus callosum. The outer part of the cerebrum is called the cerebral cortex. It is made up of grey matter, the cells of which are unmyelinated.

Cerebellum

The **cerebellum** is responsible for the coordination of muscular activity (balance and movement). It also helps in learning and remembering motor skills. It is located at the rear of the brain.

Medulla Oblongata

The **medulla oblongata** is the continuation of the spinal cord into the brain. It controls the heart and lungs, and is part of the autonomic nervous system.

Hypothalamus

The **hypothalamus** is the part of the brain that links the nervous system to the endocrine system. It secretes neurohormones that then stimulate or inhibit hormone production in the **pituitary gland**.

Pituitary Gland

The pituitary gland is the size of a pea and is located at the bottom of the hypothalamus. It is an endocrine gland that secretes a number of hormones that control growth, blood pressure, the thyroid gland and metabolism.

Reflexes

Not all responses are coordinated directly by the brain. Reflex actions enable an involuntary, near-instantaneous response to potentially life-threatening stimuli. Sending the signal to the brain for processing could result in valuable time being lost and damage being done.

A general reflex can be described as comprising:

1. stimulus is detected
2. sensory neurone signals to a relay neurone in the spinal column

3. response is sent via an effector (motor) neurone to the effector

4. effector carries out the response.

An example of a reflex response is pulling the hand away when a sharp object is accidentally touched.

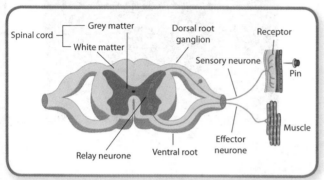

There are a wide variety of reflexes, including the blink, knee jerk and gag reflexes.

The spinal cord is made up of **white matter**, which contains myelinated nerves (sensory and effector). The central portion, which has an H shape, is the **grey matter** and is made up of many unmyelinated nerve cells. Like the grey matter in the cerebral cortex, the cells are responsible for control of the body's responses.

Knee Jerk Reflex

The knee jerk reflex, or patellar reflex, helps maintain posture and balance. Most of the time we are not aware of it operating. When the knee is struck by a hammer it can be triggered, leading to the leg kicking forwards.

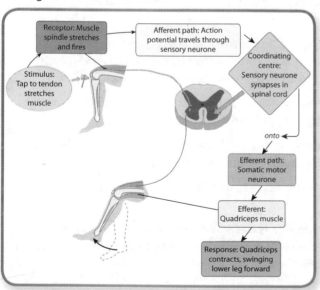

Blink Reflex

The blink reflex operates to prevent damage to the eye from objects flying into it. The stimulus is detected by the cornea, eyelids and the skin around the eyes. The ophthalmic nerve sends the signal to a relay neurone in the spinal cord which then sends the response to close the eye (blink) via an effector neurone called the facial nerve. This causes the muscles connected to the eyelids to contract. This prevents damage to the eye.

Coordination of Responses

The nervous and endocrine systems work together to coordinate responses. The hypothalamus plays a key role in this coordination.

The Hypothalamus

The hypothalamus monitors hormone levels and indirectly regulates many functions, such as fluid and food intake, sleep and body temperature. The hormones produced in the hypothalamus are called **neurohormones**. They are produced in neurosecretory cells, which resemble neurones. The cell body produces the hormone and transports it as droplets along the axon. It is then released into the blood in response to nerve impulses.

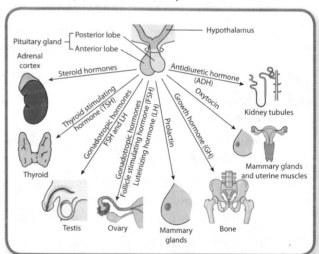

The neurohormones pass into the capillary bed in the anterior pituitary gland. The anterior pituitary gland is glandular, meaning that it makes its own hormones. The neurohormones from the hypothalamus stimulate the production of peptide hormones. These include growth hormone and hormones that influence the thyroid gland and adrenal glands.

The posterior pituitary is an extension of the hypothalamus. The neurosecretory cell axons pass through to the capillary bed in the posterior pituitary. Antidiuretic hormone (ADH) and oxytocin are stored and released into the blood.

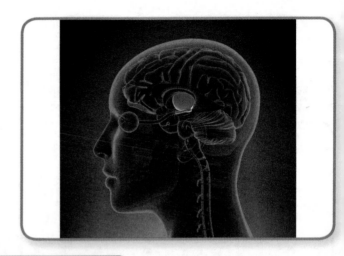

SUMMARY

- Structurally the nervous system is organised into the central and peripheral nervous systems (CNS and PNS).

- It can also be organised according to function into the somatic and autonomic nervous systems.

- The somatic nervous system is part of the peripheral nervous system and is associated with voluntary control of movement.

- Electrical impulses are sent along sensory neurones from receptors in sense organs. The impulses are received by the brain and spinal cord, processed and a response sent via effector neurones.

- The autonomic nervous system controls all bodily functions not under conscious control, including breathing, heart rate, digestion and hormone production.

- The brain is protected by thick bones in the skull and is divided into the left and right hemispheres.

- The cerebrum is the outer surface of the brain, controlling perception, voluntary movement and learning.

- The outer part of the cerebrum is the cerebral cortex, which is made up of grey matter (unmyelinated cells).

- The cerebellum coordinates muscular activity (balance and movement), learning and remembering motor skills. The medulla oblongata is the continuation of the spinal cord into the brain. It controls the heart and lungs and is part of the autonomic nervous system.

- The hypothalamus links the nervous and endocrine systems. It secretes neurohormones that then stimulate or inhibit hormone production in the pituitary gland.

- The pituitary gland is a pea-sized gland at the base of the hypothalamus. It secretes a variety of hormones controlling growth, blood pressure, the thyroid gland and metabolism.

- Reflex actions enable an involuntary, near-instantaneous response to potentially life-threatening situations.

- A general (spinal) reflex can be summarised as: stimulus is detected, sensory neurone signals to a relay neurone in the spine, response is sent via an effector (motor) neurone to the effector and the effector carries out the response. Examples include the knee jerk and blink reflexes.

● The hypothalamus monitors hormone levels and indirectly regulates many functions. Neurohormones are produced in neurone-like neurosecretory cells. The cell body produces the neurohormone which is transported as droplets along the axon. They are released in the blood and pass into the capillary bed of the pituitary gland.

● Peptide hormones are produced, including growth hormone and hormones influencing the thyroid and adrenal glands.

QUICK TEST

1. Aside from the central and peripheral nervous systems, in what other ways can the nervous system be categorised?

2. Which system controls involuntary movement?

3. Where on the brain is the cerebrum?

4. What does the cerebral cortex control?

5. Where is the medulla oblongata?

6. What does the medulla oblongata control?

7. Where is the pituitary gland found and how big is it?

8. What type of chemical does the hypothalamus secrete?

9. Summarise a reflex action.

10. What does the pituitary gland control?

PRACTICE QUESTIONS

1. A person accidentally pricks their skin on a nail, causing a withdrawal reflex.

   a) What is the role of the the muscles and glands in simple reflexes?   [2 marks]

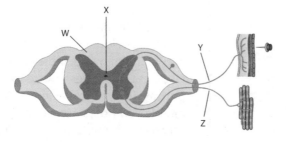

   b) Look at the diagram.

      i) Complete the missing labels W, X, Y and Z.   [4 marks]

      ii) Describe the structure and function of W and X.   [4 marks]

   c) What is the advantage of having a reflex?   [2 marks]

Muscle Action

An example of the joint coordination of the nervous and endocrine systems is the production of the hormone adrenaline. Environmental stimuli can trigger the production of adrenaline and lead to a **fight-or-flight response** in an animal. This is a response to a perceived harmful event.

The brain processes the sensory input and sends a neural signal to the hypothalamus. The hypothalamus produces a neurohormone (adrenocorticotropic hormone or ACTH) that passes into the blood and is transported to the adrenal glands. ACTH stimulates the adrenal glands to release stored adrenaline into the bloodstream and also causes more of the hormone to be made. Adrenaline is a **first messenger** hormone, triggering a number of other hormones and responses in the body. Adrenaline binds to receptors on liver cells, causing a conformational (shape) change and activating the receptors. This activates adenylate cyclase, which allows ATP to bind to the complex. Adenylate cyclase breaks ATP into a molecule called cyclic AMP (or cAMP). The cyclic AMP activates a protein kinase and the breakdown of glycogen into glucose.

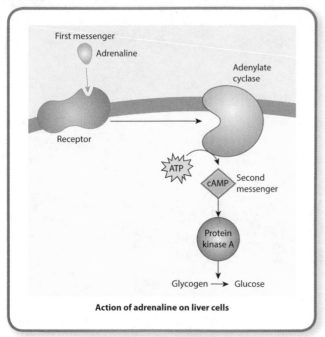

Action of adrenaline on liver cells

The cyclic AMP is classed as a **second messenger**. The process from ACTH being produced from the hypothalamus through to cyclic AMP production is an example of **cell signalling**.

Effects of Hormones and Nervous Mechanisms

Hormones such as adrenaline cause physiological responses in the body. Heart rate increases to pump more blood around the body, blood pressure is increased, the volume of air breathed in increases, the flow of blood is diverted from less essential processes to the muscles and glycogen is converted into glucose, as shown.

These processes can be measured experimentally. For example, heart rate can be measured by counting the pulse rate. This can be taken using sensors connected to a data logger. Comparing pulse rate before and after an experiment enables comparisons between the normal heart rate and the rate after exercise or a shock.

Sensors can measure changes to blood pressure as well as electrical activity of the heart.

Muscle

Many nervous signals are sent to muscle cells when they perform a movement or carry out a response. There are three types of muscle: **skeletal**, **involuntary** and **cardiac**.

Skeletal Muscle

Skeletal muscle is muscle that is attached to bones by tendons (fibres made of collagen) in the body. It responds to messages sent by the nervous system under conscious control. Skeletal muscle is comprised of bundles of muscle fibre cells called **fascicles**. The fascicles themselves, covered with a layer called the **perimysium**, are collected together to form the muscle. A protective covering of connective tissue called the epimysium surrounds and separates the muscle from other muscles. Numerous blood vessels run through the muscle to supply all the cells with oxygen and glucose.

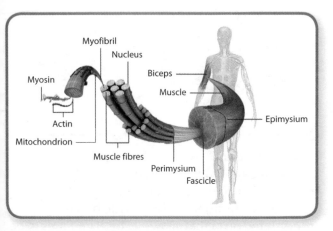

Skeletal muscle fibre is called **striated**. This is because, when viewed under the microscope, clear banding can be seen.

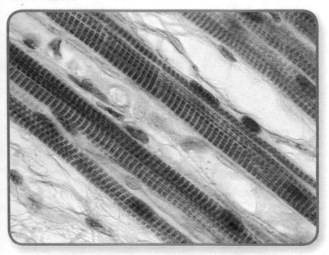

A muscle fibre comprises a number of filaments called **myofibrils**. These are made from repeating units called **sarcomeres**. The proteins making up a sarcomere are **myosin**, which is a thick filament, and **actin**, which is a thin filament.

The myosin has myosin heads that, when ATP is supplied, move and attach to the actin fibres, forming a cross bridge. When the inorganic phosphate produced from the hydrolysis of ATP is released it causes the head to pivot and initiate a power stroke, in which the actin is moved. ATP reattaches to the head, weakening the link between the myosin and actin, causing the cross bridge to break. This is known as the **sliding filament theory**.

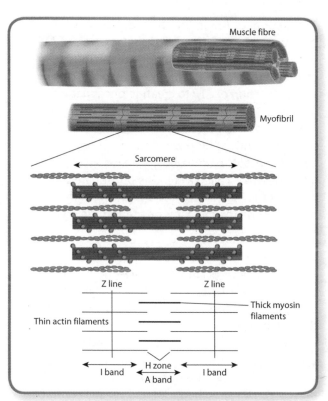

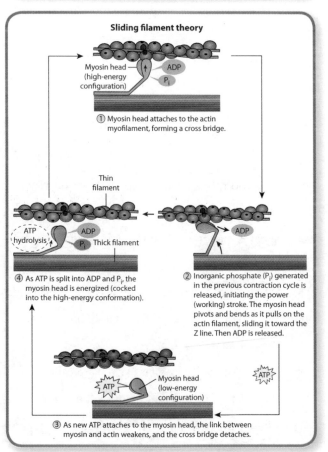

Sliding filament theory

① Myosin head attaches to the actin myofilament, forming a cross bridge.

② Inorganic phosphate (P_i) generated in the previous contraction cycle is released, initiating the power (working) stroke. The myosin head pivots and bends as it pulls on the actin filament, sliding it toward the Z line. Then ADP is released.

③ As new ATP attaches to the myosin head, the link between myosin and actin weakens, and the cross bridge detaches.

④ As ATP is split into ADP and P_i, the myosin head is energized (cocked into the high-energy conformation).

The amount of ATP in the striated muscle is maintained by **creatine phosphate**. Levels of ATP are high inside the mitochondria of the muscle cells, whereas levels of creatine phosphate are low. The conversion of ATP to creatine phosphate is favoured. The creatine phosphate diffuses from the mitochondria to the myofibril. Once in the myofibril, the level of ADP is high when the myofibril has contracted, so creatine phosphate is converted back into ATP. This is called a creatine phosphate shuttle: it moves the high-energy phosphate from the mitochondria to where it is needed, in the myofibril.

Involuntary Muscle

Involuntary muscle, or smooth muscle, is non-striated. The contractions of smooth muscle move materials through the alimentary canal and regulate the diameters of blood vessels. It is found in the walls of the gut, blood vessels, lymphatic vessels, bladder, male and female reproductive tracts and the iris of the eye. This type of muscle can contract and relax but has a much wider range than striated muscle. Thus the muscle can be stretched a lot and yet still contract. As with striated muscle, involuntary muscle is made of actin and myosin fibres.

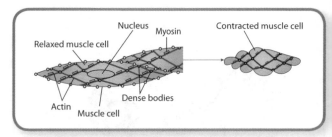

Cardiac Muscle

Cardiac muscle is found only in the heart. Cardiac muscle is striated muscle that is under involuntary control. It differs from striated muscle by having **intercalated discs** that allow electrical impulses to be sent rapidly to enable coordinated contractions. The gaps between discs are connected by **desmosomes**, which anchor the discs together, and gap junctions, connecting the cytoplasm of the muscle cells.

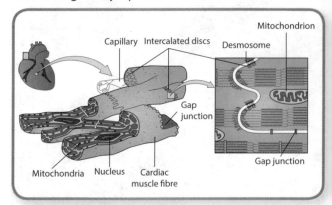

QUICK TEST

1. What hormone is produced by the hypothalamus in response to the detection of a perceived threat?

2. On what gland does this hormone have an effect?

3. What is meant when adrenaline is said to be a first messenger hormone?

4. What chemical is ATP converted to when adrenaline binds to receptors on kidney cells?

5. What does the chemical named in question 4 do in the liver?

6. What type of muscle is found in blood vessels?

7. What are fascicles?

8. Name the two types of muscle filament forming a sarcomere.

9. What is the role of creatine phosphate in muscle?

10. What is the function of intercalated discs in cardiac muscle?

SUMMARY

- Adrenaline is a hormone produced through the cooperation of the nervous and endocrine systems. A perceived threat can trigger the production of adrenaline and lead to a fight-or-flight response. The physiological effects of adrenaline include an increase in heart rate, blood pressure, volume of air breathed in and blood flow is diverted from less essential processes.

- The brain processes the sensory input and sends a neural signal to the hypothalamus. The hypothalamus produces adrenocorticotropic hormone (ACTH), which passes to the adrenal gland. ACTH stimulates the adrenal gland to release stored adrenaline into the blood and produce more.

- Adrenaline is a first messenger hormone that triggers the release of other hormones. Adrenaline binds to receptors on liver cells, causing conformational changes and activating the receptors.

- Adenylate cyclase allows ATP to bind to the complex, breaking it down into cyclic AMP. Cyclic AMP, a second messenger, activates a protein kinase and the breakdown of glycogen into glucose.

- The process of ACTH being produced by the hypothalamus through the cyclic AMP production is an example of cell signalling.

- There are three types of muscle, skeletal, involuntary and cardiac.

- Skeletal muscle is attached to bones by tendons and responds to messages under conscious control. It is striated (striped) when observed under a microscope.

- A muscle fibre is made up of myofibrils, each made from repeating sarcomeres containing the protein filaments myosin (thick) and actin (thin).

- ATP causes the myosin heads to attach to actin filaments, forming a cross bridge. When P_i is released, the head pivots and initiates a power stroke, moving the actin (contraction). Levels of ATP in muscle are maintained by creatine phosphate in the mitochondria and muscle. The creatine phosphate shuttle ensures that high-energy phosphate is moved into mitochondria when needed.

- Involuntary (smooth) muscle is non-striated and found in walls of vessels. The muscle can contract and relax over a much wider range than striated muscle.

- Cardiac muscle is only found in the heart and is striated muscle under involuntary control.

- Intercalated discs are present that enable electrical impulses to be sent rapidly throughout the heart. This enables coordinated contractions. The gaps between cardiac muscles are connected by desmosomes which anchor the discs together and gap junctions which connect the cytoplasm of the muscle cells.

PRACTICE QUESTIONS

1. **a)** Which of the following is unique to cardiac muscle?

    A It is non-striated. ☐

    B It is has intercalated discs. ☐

    C It contains smooth muscle tissue. ☐

    D It is involuntary. ☐

    [1 mark]

    b) What is a bundle of muscle fibres called? [1 mark]

    c) Describe how creatine phosphate maintains the level of ATP in striated muscle. [4 marks]

Skeletal Tissues

Humans have an endoskeleton, an internal skeleton. The skeleton consists of a variety of different tissues.

Cartilage

Cartilage is a flexible connective tissue that is found in a variety of different locations in humans. It is not as hard or as rigid as bone but is stiffer and less flexible than muscle. It can be found covering the ends of bones in a joint, in the ear and nose, the rib cage and in the bronchioles in the lungs.

There are three types of cartilage: hyaline, yellow elastic and white fibrous.

Hyaline Cartilage

Hyaline cartilage is the most abundant type of cartilage in the human body. It is present in the bronchi, nose and trachea and covers the surface of bones. Its function is to provide a smooth surface so tissues can move or slide easily over each other. It consists of a bluish-white shiny elastic material along with a matrix of **chondroitin sulfate**. Chondroitin sulfate has many fine collagen fibres embedded in it and contains large numbers of **chondrocytes**, the only cell type found in cartilage. Chondrocytes maintain healthy cartilage, producing the matrix. The cartilage has a covering called a **perichondrium**, which is a dense membrane wrapping the cartilage.

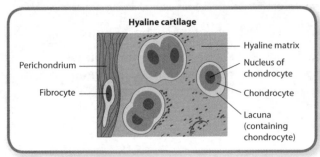

Hyaline cartilage

Perichondrium
Fibrocyte
Hyaline matrix
Nucleus of chondrocyte
Chondrocyte
Lacuna (containing chondrocyte)

Yellow Elastic Cartilage

Yellow elastic cartilage is a yellowish colour. Its function is to provide support to surrounding structures. It also helps to define and maintain the shape of the body part in which it is found. It is present in the ear and nose. The chondrocytes sit in a threadlike network of elastic fibres in the matrix. Yellow elastic cartilage, like hyaline cartilage, has a perichondrium.

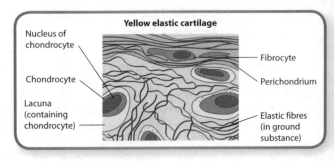

Yellow elastic cartilage

Nucleus of chondrocyte
Chondrocyte
Lacuna (containing chondrocyte)
Fibrocyte
Perichondrium
Elastic fibres (in ground substance)

White Fibrous Cartilage

White fibrous cartilage is a tough form of cartilage with dense bundles of collagen fibres in the matrix. The chondrocytes are scattered along the fibres in rows. Unlike the other forms of cartilage, there is no perichondrium. White fibrous cartilage is found in the discs between vertebrae and the pads of the knee joint. It also occurs where the hip bones join at the front of the body.

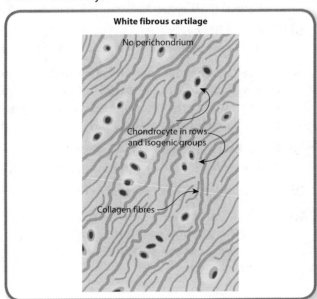

White fibrous cartilage

No perichondrium
Chondrocyte in rows and isogenic groups
Collagen fibres

Bone

Bone is an organ that is rigid. It makes up part of the human skeleton. The function of bone is to protect the internal organs and provide support. It is also the site of red and white blood cell production and it stores minerals too. The bone in the human skeleton is either **compact bone** or **cancellous bone**. Compact bone makes up around 80% of the human skeleton. It is comprised of a matrix that is approximately 30% organic and 70% inorganic. The organic portion is mainly collagen, which gives the bone a level of fracture resistance. The inorganic component is mainly the compound **hydroxyapatite**, which contains calcium and phosphate. It gives the bone its rigidity. Compact bone is denser than cancellous bone, which is spongy in nature.

Bone Formation and Reformation

Bone is a living organ. It is constantly being broken down and reformed by specialised cells called **osteoblasts** and **osteoclasts**. Osteoblasts are located in the bone matrix and deposit the inorganic component of the matrix whereas osteoclasts absorb bone tissue during growth and healing.

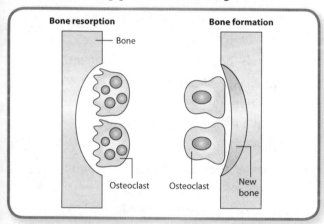

The Haversian System

The **osteon** is the functional unit in compact bone. The **Haversian system** consists of cylindrical structures comprising concentric layers that surround

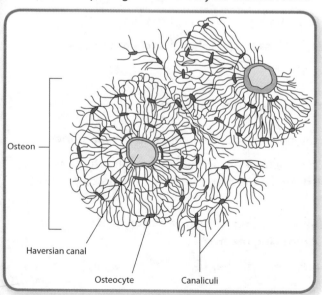

a central Haversian canal. Some osteoblasts develop into osteocytes. These then live in a small space, the lacuna (plural: lacunae). The osteocytes are connected to other osteocytes via a network of canaliculi (canal-like passages). This allows the osteocytes to exchange nutrients and waste. Further, larger channels called Volkmann's channels connect the osteons together.

Disorders of Bone

Bone development can be affected through a deficiency of any of the elements needed for bone manufacture. Most of the minerals needed for bone growth are found naturally in the diet. However, certain key deficiencies can lead to problems.

Calcium Deficiency

Calcium is essential for bone growth. It is a key element in the formation of hydroxyapatite. As well as being needed for the growth of bones, calcium is also required for the nervous system to function correctly and for muscle contraction. The calcium comes from food in the diet: i.e. fish, beans and dairy products such as milk, yoghurt and cheese. If there is not enough, then the body takes its calcium from the bones. This can cause a condition called osteomalacia.

Osteomalacia

Osteomalacia is a disease occurring in adults. The consequence of calcium being reabsorbed by the body from the bones leads to symptoms such as pain across the whole body, muscle weakness and bone fragility. It is caused by a diet poor in calcium and by vitamin D deficiency. Vitamin D is formed in the skin on exposure to sunlight. It is an essential vitamin that attaches to a receptor in the plasma membrane of osteoblasts and osteoclasts. Vitamin D is needed for the absorption of calcium from the intestine during digestion. If it is absent then less calcium is taken up and the body starts to use the calcium present in bone.

Rickets

Vitamin D deficiency or calcium deficiency in childhood can lead to rickets, which is the childhood version of osteomalacia. It is far more serious than osteomalacia due to the bones being affected at a time of major growth. A child with rickets will have defective calcification of the bones. This can lead to a wide range of symptoms including skeletal deformities such as bowed legs.

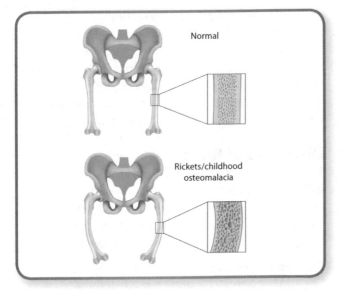

Normal

Rickets/childhood osteomalacia

Osteoporosis

Osteoporosis is a disease that causes brittle bones, thus increasing the chance of bone fractures. It is typically caused by hormonal changes in later life, which is why older females are more at risk than older males. Deficiency in calcium or vitamin D can also have an effect. Unlike osteomalacia, which has visible symptoms, osteoporosis has no real symptoms until a bone breaks. A reduction in height can indicate that a person has osteoporosis because the spinal vertebrae become weak and compressed, which can cause them to fracture. It is the most common cause of broken bones in older women. Treatment and prevention focuses on changing the diet to increase calcium absorption and medication to increase bone density.

QUICK TEST

1. What is cartilage?
2. What type of cartilage covers the surface of bones?
3. What type of cartilage is found in the vertebral discs?
4. What is embedded in chondroitin sulfate to form the matrix?
5. What is the role of the perichondrium?
6. Which type of cartilage does not have a perichondrium?
7. What are the two types of bone?
8. What is hydroxyapatite?
9. What are the roles of osteoblasts and osteoclasts?
10. What is the cause of osteomalacia?

SUMMARY

- The human skeleton is an endoskeleton comprised of a range of different tissues.

- Cartilage is a flexible connective tissue; it is stiffer and less flexible than muscle but not as rigid as bone.

- There are three types of cartilage:
  - hyaline: in the bronchi, nose and trachea and covers the surface of bones
  - yellow elastic: found in the ear and nose
  - white fibrous: in the discs between vertebrae, the pads of the knee joint and the hip bones.

- Hyaline cartilage provides a smooth surface so tissues can move or slide over each other easily. It consists of a bluish-white shiny elastic material along with a matrix formed from chondroitin sulfate.

- Chondroitin sulfate has many collagen fibres embedded along with large numbers of chondrocytes, which maintain healthy cartilage, producing the matrix.

- Perichondrium is a dense membrane that surrounds the cartilage.

- Yellow elastic cartilage supports surrounding structures and defines and maintains shape. Chondrocytes are present in a threadlike network of elastic fibres in the matrix. Yellow elastic cartilage is surrounded by a perichondrium.

- White fibrous cartilage has no perichondrium, and is tough with dense bundles of collagen fibres within a matrix. Chondrocytes are scattered along the fibres in rows.

- Bone is a rigid organ that protects internal organs, provides support, stores minerals and produces red and white blood cells. There are two types of bone: 80% of bone in the body is compact bone and 20% is cancellous bone.

- Compact bone is made of a matrix 30% organic material (collagen) to give a level of fracture resistance. The inorganic material, mainly hydroxyapatite containing calcium and phosphate gives the bone its rigidity.

- Bone is a living organ that is constantly being broken down and reformed by osteoblasts and osteoclasts. Osteoblasts in the bone matrix deposit the inorganic part of the matrix. Osteoclasts reabsorb bone tissue during growth and healing.

- The Haversian system comprises cylindrical structures with concentric layers surrounding a central canal.

- Some osteoblasts develop into osteocytes in a lacuna, connected to other osteocytes via canaliculi.

- Bone disorders can occur when elements necessary for growth are missing.

- Calcium deficiency leads to osteomalacia, a disease in adults, where the calcium in bones is reabsorbed.

- Vitamin D is essential for the absorption of calcium from the intestine, if absent, bone calcium is removed. Vitamin D deficiency in childhood leads to rickets, the childhood form of osteomalacia. As a child's bones are still growing, the consequences of rickets are more severe, such as bowed legs.

- Osteoporosis is caused by hormonal changes in later life and causes bones to become brittle. It is the most common cause of broken bones in older people.

PRACTICE QUESTIONS

1. Osteomalacia is a disease that occurs in adults. It is caused by calcium being reabsorbed from the bones.

   a) What are the symptoms of osteomalacia? **[2 marks]**

   b) What are two causes of osteomalacia? **[2 marks]**

   c) The bone is a rigid organ; 70% of compact bone is made up of hydroxyapatite. Explain how osteomalacia affects hydroxyapatite. **[2 marks]**

   d) The diagram shows the Haversian system.

      Name the structures X, Y and Z. **[3 marks]**

   e) What is the childhood form of osteomalacia? Why are its consequences more severe than those of osteomalacia?

      [4 marks]

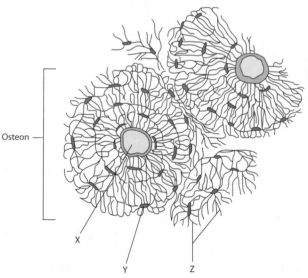

Osteon

X

Y   Z

The Skeleton

The portion of the skeleton consisting of bone or cartilage that supports the appendages is called the **appendicular skeleton** (see figure).

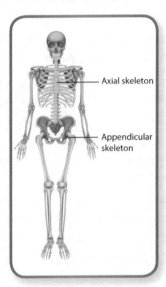

Axial skeleton

Appendicular skeleton

The forelimbs (the arms) are attached to the pectoral, or shoulder, girdle whereas the hind limbs (legs) are connected to the pelvic girdle.

Bones of the head and the trunk form the **axial skeleton**. In humans this consists of around 80 bones.

Broken Bones

There are a variety of different ways by which bones can break or fracture. **Displaced fractures** are when the bone snaps in two or more parts and moves so that the ends are no longer straight. With a non-displaced fracture, the bone cracks part way or all the way through, but does not move and so maintains its original alignment.

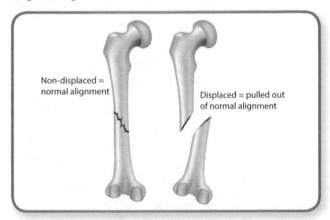

Non-displaced = normal alignment

Displaced = pulled out of normal alignment

An open fracture is where the bone breaks through the skin. Sometimes it will recede back into the wound and not be visible. A closed fracture is when the bone breaks but does not break through the skin. Open fractures are more risky as there is a chance of the bone becoming infected.

The severity of the fracture depends on the location and the damage done to the bone and the tissue near it. If the blood vessels or nerves are damaged or the bone or surrounding tissues become infected, then the consequences are more severe.

Vertebral Column

The vertebral column, or spine, is part of the axial skeleton. It consists of a series of segmented bones called vertebrae which enclose and protect the spinal cord. Humans have 33 vertebrae. The vertebrae are separated by vertebral discs that are made of cartilage and form a **fibrocartilaginous joint**. This allows some movement of the spine so the person can move and twist their body without breaking the spinal cord. It also holds the vertebrae together and acts as a shock absorber.

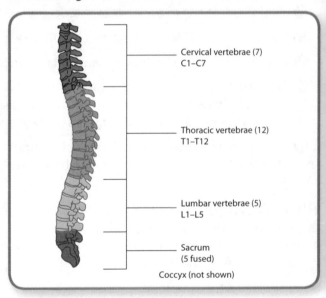

Cervical vertebrae (7)
C1–C7

Thoracic vertebrae (12)
T1–T12

Lumbar vertebrae (5)
L1–L5

Sacrum
(5 fused)

Coccyx (not shown)

The **cervical vertebrae** are at the top of the spinal column, in the neck. They support the head and allow it to move.

Thoracic vertebrae are connected to the rib cage in the thorax. They are attached to the ribs and also help support the upper body.

The **lumbar vertebrae** are the five vertebrae in the lower back between the thoracic vertebrae and the sacrum. They are the largest vertebrae and carry all of the upper body weight while allowing movement and flexibility of the trunk.

The **sacrum** is a triangular bone formed from five fused vertebrae. Its main function is to support the weight of the body and to connect the axial skeleton with the lower appendicular skeleton through the pelvis.

Postural Deformities

The spine of a healthy individual has gentle curves. This is so that the spine can absorb stresses from gravity and body movement. Deformities of the spine cause the natural curvature of the spine to become misaligned or exaggerated.

Scoliosis

Scoliosis is a condition where the spine curves laterally instead of maintaining a natural straight line. Viewed from the front or back, the spine appears to be curved.

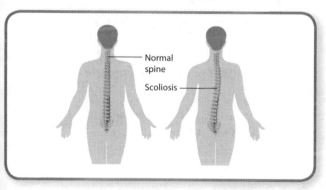

Normal spine
Scoliosis

There are a number of causes of scoliosis. People with abnormal muscles or nerves can develop the condition, e.g. sufferers of spina bifida or cerebral palsy. Sometimes the cause can be an accident, leading to collapse of the bones. Major back surgery can lead to the condition forming. Some sufferers of **osteoporosis** may develop it.

Treatment can be through wearing back braces, particularly in children who may have inherited a condition. If the bones have not matured they can be affected by this treatment. Surgery is an option to reduce the effect of the condition, although it is difficult to correct completely. Metal rods can be inserted and vertebrae fused together to minimise lateral misalignment.

Kyphosis

Kyphosis is a condition where the thoracic region of the spine can become excessively curved, causing a hunched back.

Kyphosis is most commonly caused by osteoporosis, in which the vertebrae fracture at the front. The rear part of the vertebra retains its height, so the vertebrae are shifted forwards. Kyphosis with a genetic basis can be treated through surgery. If the cause is osteoporosis then treating the cause of the osteoporosis may help to ease the symptoms of kyphosis. Surgery is not recommended with adults suffering from kyphosis. Sufferers are taught instead to cope with the condition.

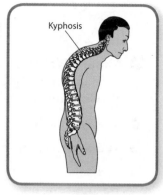

Kyphosis

Joints

There are a number of joints in the skeleton. A joint is where two or more bones meet.

Fixed joints or fibrous joints are held together by only a ligament (fibrous connective tissue that connects bone to bone). Examples include the plates of the skull and the teeth, which are held to their bony sockets.

Cartilaginous joints are where cartilage connects the articulating bones, e.g. the vertebrae in the spine.

Synovial joints are the most common joints in the body. They have a synovial capsule surrounding the entire joint. The synovial capsule includes a synovial membrane that secretes synovial fluid. Hyaline cartilage is present, padding the ends of the bones.

Types of synovial joint are shown in the figure.

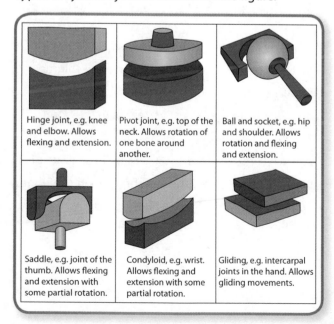

Hinge joint, e.g. knee and elbow. Allows flexing and extension.

Pivot joint, e.g. top of the neck. Allows rotation of one bone around another.

Ball and socket, e.g. hip and shoulder. Allows rotation and flexing and extension.

Saddle, e.g. joint of the thumb. Allows flexing and extension with some partial rotation.

Condyloid, e.g. wrist. Allows flexing and extension with some partial rotation.

Gliding, e.g. intercarpal joints in the hand. Allows gliding movements.

SUMMARY

- The appendicular skeleton is the portion of the skeleton that supports the appendages. The forelimbs are attached to the pectoral, or shoulder, girdle. The hind limbs are attached to the pelvic girdle.

- The axial skeleton comprises approximately 80 bones of the head and the trunk of the body.

- There are a number of types of broken bone (fracture).

- In displaced fractures the bone snaps and moves so the ends are not straight. In non-displaced fractures the bone does not move. An open fracture is where the bone breaks through the skin and is more prone to infection. A closed fracture is where the breakage does not pierce the skin.

- The vertebral column, or spine, is a series of segmented bones called vertebrae, which enclose and protect the spinal cord. Humans have 33 vertebrae separated by vertebral discs made of cartilage, forming a cartilaginous joint that allows movement and acts as a shock absorber.

- The vertebral column is divided into four sections: cervical, thoracic, lumbar and sacral.

- Postural deformities occur through disease or damage.

- Scoliosis is where the spine curves laterally. It is caused by accident or abnormal muscle or nerves. Back braces and eventual surgery are ways to treat the disorder.

- Kyphosis is where the thoracic vertebrae become excessively curved (a hunched back). This is most commonly caused by osteoporosis, in which the front part of the vertebrae fractures.

QUICK TEST

1. What is the name of the part of the skeleton supporting the arms and legs?
2. What type of fracture occurs when bone snaps in two or more parts and move so the ends are not straight?
3. Why are open fractures more of a risk than closed fractures?
4. What is the function of the vertebral column or spine?
5. The vertebral column can be divided into four sections. What are they?
6. Which are the largest vertebrae in the body?
7. What is scoliosis?
8. Why are skeletal disorders more of an issue in children than in adults?
9. What happens to the vertebrae when someone suffers from kyphosis?
10. What type of joint is in (a) the wrist and (b) the knee?

PRACTICE QUESTIONS

1. Look at the diagram of the spinal column.

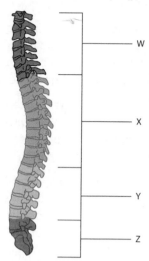

a) What are sections W, X, Y and Z? [4 marks]

b) Scoliosis is a disorder affecting the spine.
Draw the spine of someone suffering from scoliosis. [2 marks]

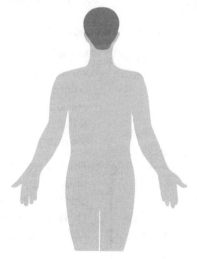

c) Give two typical treatments for scoliosis. [2 marks]

Photosynthesis

Photosynthesis is the conversion of carbon dioxide and water by plants into glucose, using energy from sunlight. The energy in sunlight is trapped by a pigment called chlorophyll in the leaves and the energy transferred into the chemical bonds between atoms in glucose.

$$\text{Carbon dioxide + water} \xrightarrow[\text{Light energy}]{\text{Chlorophyll}} \text{glucose + oxygen}$$

This equation is a summary of the process of photosynthesis. It shows what raw materials are needed and what products are produced. It is important to realise that the process of photosynthesis is more complex than shown here, with a number of enzyme-catalysed reactions taking place.

Chloroplasts

Photosynthesis takes place inside organelles called **chloroplasts**. Chloroplasts have a prokaryotic origin. They are thought to have originated from cyanobacteria, a type of bacterium that can photosynthesise, which became a permanent part of plant cells through **endosymbiosis** approximately 600 million years ago. Evidence for this includes the fact that the chloroplast contains its own DNA.

Chloroplast Structure

The chloroplast's structure enables it to carry out the different stages of photosynthesis in the same organelle.

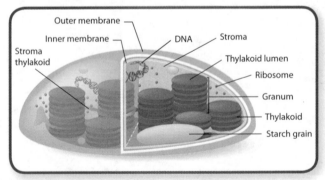

The chloroplast has an outer membrane that is made of a phospholipid bilayer.

The inside of the chloroplast is filled with a colourless fluid called the **stroma**. A number of chemical reactions take place in the stroma, called the light-independent reactions.

Within the stroma are stacks of sac-like **thylakoids**. Thylakoids are membrane-bound organelles within the chloroplast itself. This is where the light-dependent reactions of photosynthesis take place.

Thylakoid Structure

Thylakoids have a thylakoid membrane which surrounds a fluid-filled space, called the thylakoid lumen.

The thylakoids form a stack of discs called a **granum**. Collections of the stacks are called grana.

Connecting the granum stacks together are **stroma thylakoids** (also know as lamellae), which ensure the grana work together as one unit.

Photosynthetic Pigments

Pigments are compounds that reflect certain wavelengths of light. This makes the pigments appear colourful. Flowers, animal skin and paints all contain coloured pigments. The wavelengths that are not reflected are absorbed and this is why they are useful for photosynthetic organisms.

There is a wide range of pigments used in photosynthesis. The most common are the chlorophylls, the most important being chlorophyll *a*. This is a greenish pigment, absorbing blue wavelengths (425–450 nm) and red wavelengths (600–700 nm) and reflecting green (500–550 nm).

Phytochrome is a blue-green pigment found in many plants. It regulates photomorphogenesis, the development of structures in plants in response to light. This is different to photosynthesis.

The different photosynthetic pigments can be separated experimentally using thin layer chromatography.

Light-harvesting Systems

Complexes of chlorophylls and carotenoid proteins form **light-harvesting systems**. The molecules get excited when a photon of light collides with them. The excited molecule transfers the excitation energy to an adjacent molecule. In this way, the energy is passed from molecule to molecule along the light-harvesting system.

Photosystems

There are two photosystems involved in photosynthesis. Photosystems combine the light-harvesting system with other proteins to transfer excitation energy and electrons.

Photosystem I (or PSI) was the first to be discovered, but it is not the start of the photosynthetic sequence. Its reactions take place in the stroma of the thylakoid.

Photosystem II (or PSII) is the starting point for photosynthesis. The reactions take place inside the lumen of the thylakoid.

Both photosystems comprise the light-dependent stage of photosynthesis.

Light-dependent Stage of Photosynthesis

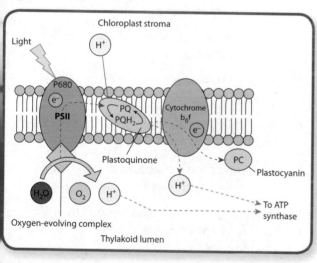

Photons of light excite chlorophyll in the photosystem II (PSII) complex. The excitation drives the breakdown of water to form oxygen gas and hydrogen ions (protons). The two electrons released pass through the PSII complex into the space between the phosphate

heads of the phospholipid bilayer to an electron-accepting molecule called plastoquinone. This is reduced by the two electrons, forming plastoquinol (PQ). The electrons pass down an electron transport chain to a molecule of cytochrome and then plastocyanin. This also helps to create a proton gradient from a high concentration in the thylakoid lumen to a low concentration in the stroma.

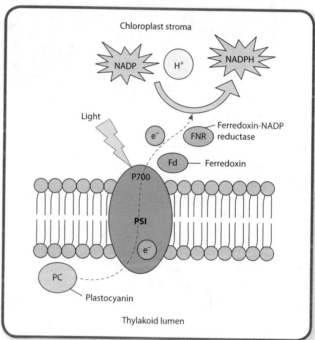

The electrons released by plastoquinol feed into photosystem I (PSI). The electrons are again excited by light, increasing their energy level. Membrane-bound proteins then transfer the electrons to drive the conversion of two molecules of the coenzyme NADP with two protons to form NADPH. NADPH is a reducing agent that can pass electrons to other molecules.

$$2NADP + 2H^+ \rightarrow 2NADPH_2$$

The light-dependent stage of photosynthesis resembles a Z shape in terms of the stepwise energy increase gained by electrons. This can be summarised as shown in the next figure.

Electron transport chain

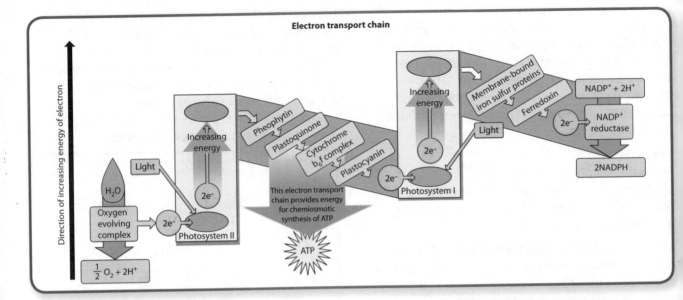

ATP Synthesis

The high concentration of protons in the thylakoid lumen enables the generation of ATP. The protons pass through ATP synthase, which causes ADP and inorganic phosphate ions (P_i) to form ATP. This also helps maintain the proton gradient from high in the thylakoid lumen to low in the chloroplast stroma.

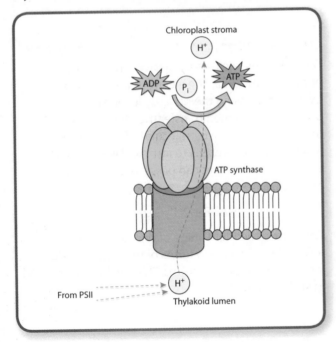

QUICK TEST

1. Where do the reactions of photosynthesis take place?

2. What is the stroma?

3. Draw and label a diagram of a cross section through a chloroplast.

4. What wavelengths of light do the pigment chlorophyll *a* absorb?

5. What are the main components of a light-harvesting system?

6. With which photosystem does photosynthesis start?

7. What drives the breakdown of water into oxygen and hydrogen ions?

8. How many electrons pass through the PSII complex to plastoquinone, reducing it to plastoquinol?

9. In PSI, what is NADP converted into?

10. What molecule in the thylakoid membrane produces ATP?

- Photosynthesis can be represented by the following equation:

$$\text{Carbon dioxide + water} \xrightarrow[\text{Light energy}]{\text{Chlorophyll}} \text{glucose + oxygen}$$

- Chloroplasts are organelles with a prokaryotic origin and are the site of photosynthesis.

- The outer chloroplast membrane is a phospholipid bilayer. Within is a colourless liquid called the stroma where the light-independent reactions take place. In the stroma are stacks of sac-like thylakoids where the light-dependent reactions take place.

- The thylakoids are membrane-bound organelles of the chloroplast. Thylakoids form stacks of discs called grana.

- A number of pigments are present in a chloroplast, including the chlorophylls. Chlorophyll a absorbs light with wavelengths of 425–450 nm (blue) and 600–700 nm (red). Green light with a wavelength of 500–550 nm is reflected.

- Complexes of chlorophylls and carotenoid proteins form light-harvesting systems.

- The molecules get excited when a photon collides with them. The excited molecules transfer the excitation energy into adjacent molecules.

- Photosystems (PS) combine light-harvesting systems and other proteins to transfer energy and electrons. There are two photosystems in the light-dependent stage. PS I was the first to be discovered in the stroma, but is not the start of photosynthesis. PS II is the starting point and the reactions take place in the thylakoid lumen.

- Photons excite chlorophyll in the PSII complex and drive the breakdown of water to form O_2 and H^+ ions.

- Two electrons pass through the PSII complex to plastoquinone, reducing it to plastoquinol. The electrons pass down an electron transport chain to a cytochrome molecule and then plastocyanin. This creates a proton gradient from a high concentration in the stroma to a low concentration in the lumen.

- The electrons released by plastoquinol feed into PSI. The electrons are re-excited by light.

- Membrane-bound proteins then transfer the electrons to drive the conversion of two molecules of the coenzyme NADP with two electrons to form the reducing agent NADPH.

- The increased number of protons in the thylakoid pass through ATP synthase, causing ATP to form from ADP and P_i while maintaining the proton gradient.

PRACTICE QUESTIONS

1. DCMU (3-(3,4-dichlorophenyl)-1,1-dimethylurea) is a herbicide that inhibits photosynthesis. It blocks the plastoquinone-binding site in photosystem II. It blocks no other parts of the photosynthetic pathway, including light absorption and carbon fixation in the Calvin cycle.

   a) Suggest what effect DCMU would have on electron transport in photosystem II. **[2 marks]**

   b) What would the effect be on photosystem I? **[2 marks]**

Light-Independent Stage

The light-independent stage of photosynthesis includes the chemical reactions that convert carbon dioxide into glucose. In the past it was also called the dark stage of photosynthesis. However, this name is misleading, implying that it takes place in the absence of light, e.g. at night. The reactions can only take place when light is available, because the light-independent reactions depend on the products of the light-*dependent* reactions.

There are three phases during the light-independent stage, which are collectively called the **Calvin cycle**. This uses the products of the light-dependent stage, which is the reason why it cannot take place in the dark.

Calvin Cycle

It is useful to keep track of the number of carbon atoms that are chemically bonded together. The purpose of the Calvin cycle is to start with carbon dioxide, a compound containing a single carbon, and finish with glucose, a six-carbon-containing compound.

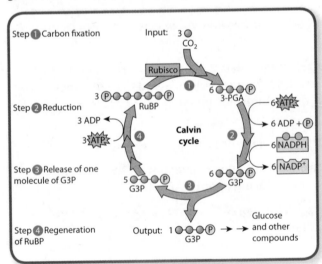

Three molecules of carbon dioxide are fed into the Calvin cycle, where it is reacted with a molecule called **ribulose bisphosphate** (RuBP, a five-carbon compound). This is catalysed by the enzyme ribulose bisphosphate carboxylase oxygenase, or Rubisco. It undergoes a series of reactions to form six molecules of a **triose phosphate** (3-phosphoglycerate or 3-PGA).

Six molecules of ATP are hydrolysed to produce ADP and P_i and six molecules of NADPH are converted back into six molecules of NADP$^+$ and six phosphate molecules. This leads to the reduction of the triose phosphate 3-PGA into six molecules of glucose 3-phosphate (G3P), another triose phosphate.

One molecule of the triose phosphate G3P leaves the cycle. It is joined to another molecule of G3P to form glucose. This can be used in respiration or to make other **organic molecules**.

The remaining five triose phosphate G3P molecules are converted into RuBP using three molecules of ATP in the process. The RuBP is then reacted with carbon dioxide and the cycle starts again.

It is important to understand that although it appears that the cycle moves in a set order, in reality each of the reactions of the cycle are taking place at the same time, as long as there is an adequate supply of carbon dioxide, ATP and NADPH (reduced NADP).

Using Triose Phosphate
The triose phosphate that leaves the Calvin cycle, G3P, is a starting material for the synthesis of a wide range of carbohydrates, lipids and amino acids. The triose phosphate is also used to replenish RuBP, which goes on to fix more CO_2.

Factors Affecting Photosynthesis
Photosynthesis is affected by a variety of different factors. A **limiting factor** is a factor that prevents the optimum rate of reaction because it is in short supply.

Carbon Dioxide Concentration
Carbon dioxide is a limiting factor for photosynthesis.

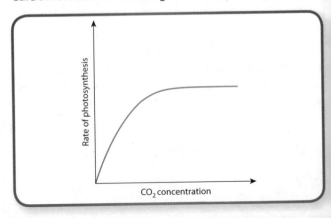

As the carbon dioxide level increases, photosynthesis increases up to the point where other factors become limiting.

Light Intensity

The light intensity is also a limiting factor in photosynthesis.

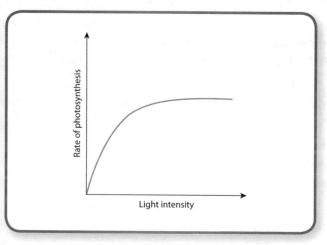

As the light intensity increases the photosystems I and II work more effectively. The rate of photosynthesis increases with increasing light intensity until another factor becomes limiting.

Temperature

Photosynthesis is controlled by enzymes. This means that it is affected by temperature. Photosynthesis will occur at its maximum rate at the optimal temperature for the enzymes involved.

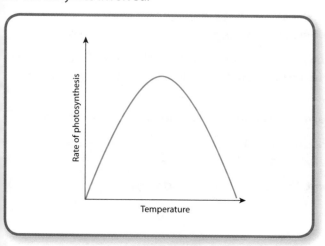

Water Levels

Water is required for photosynthesis. If water becomes limited, e.g. due to stomata closing, then photosynthesis may decline in rate or even stop.

Each stage step in the Calvin cycle is catalysed by a specific enzyme. The enzymes can be inhibited by **metabolic poisons** or by genetic mutations limiting the effectiveness of the enzymes.

At each stage of the Calvin cycle, if a metabolite becomes in short supply, then the cycle will slow and stop.

QUICK TEST

1. The light-independent phase of photosynthesis is also called the dark phase. Why is it not true to say it can take place in the dark?

2. What is the name of the cycle converting carbon dioxide into glucose?

3. What is the first molecule carbon dioxide is reacted with?

4. What enzyme catalyses this reaction?

5. What type of molecule is 3-PGA?

6. What molecules are joined together to form glucose?

7. Give two factors that limit photosynthesis.

8. How are enzymes involved in the cycle?

9. How could metabolic poisons slow or stop photosynthesis?

10. Suggest what would happen to photosynthesis if a plant was short of water.

SUMMARY

- The light-independent stage of photosynthesis includes the reactions that convert carbon dioxide into glucose. Despite the name, it can only take place when light is available.

- There are three phases of the Calvin cycle, which depend on the products from the light-dependent stage.

- The Calvin cycle starts with the input of carbon dioxide and ends with the release of glucose. Three molecules of CO_2 are fed into the cycle, where it reacts with a molecule called ribulose bisphosphate (RuBP).

- RuBP undergoes a series of reactions to form six molecules of a triose phosphate, 3-phosphoglycerate (3-PGA).

- Six molecules of ATP are hydrolysed to form ADP + P_i. Six molecules of NADPH are converted back into six molecules of $NADP^+$ and six P_i molecules.

- 3-PGA is converted into glucose 3-phosphate (G3P).

- One molecule of G3P leaves the cell and will join onto another G3P molecule to form glucose. The glucose is used for respiration or to make other organic molecules.

- The remaining five G3P molecules are converted into RuBP using three molecules of ATP. RuBP is then reacted with CO_2 by the enzyme Rubisco, starting the process again.

- Although the cycle proceeds in a set order, the reactions all take place simultaneously, as long as enough CO_2, ATP and NADPH are available.

- G3P leaving the cycle is also the starting material for a wide range of carbohydrates, lipids and amino acids.

- Photosynthesis is affected by a variety of different factors. CO_2 is required for photosynthesis and it is a limiting factor. When levels increase, other factors become limiting.

- Light intensity is also a limiting factor. As light intensity increases, PSI and PSII work more effectively and will increase until another factor becomes limiting.

- Photosynthesis is dependent on a range of enzymes so temperature affects the rate of reaction. The enzymes work best in an optimal temperature range: above and below this range the reaction will be slower.

- Water is a reactant in the light-dependent phase; if it becomes limited photosynthesis will cease.

- At each stage of the Calvin cycles specific enzymes operate. They can be inhibited by metabolic poisons or by genetic mutations that limit the effectiveness of the enzymes.

- If metabolites become short in supply at any point, the cycle will slow and stop.

PRACTICE QUESTIONS

1. A simplified version of the Calvin cycle is shown below.

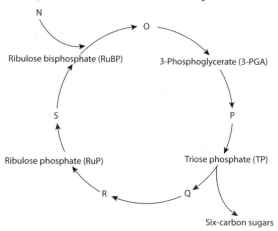

a) What is molecule N? [1 mark]

b) What stage of photosynthesis involves the Calvin cycle? [1 mark]

c) What products from the other stage of photosynthesis are required for the Calvin cycle? [2 marks]

d) Which **two** letters in the simplified version of the Calvin cycle represent steps where the chemicals named in **c)** are required? [2 marks]

e) What is the name of the enzyme that catalyses the step from ribulose bisphosphate (RuBP) to O? [1 mark]

Respiration

Respiration is the process in which energy that is stored in complex molecules is transferred to ATP. The ATP molecules are then used for metabolic processes.

Mitochondria

The mitochondria are another example of an organelle – like chloroplasts – that was originally a prokaryotic organism and that became an endosymbiont. Eventually the endosymbiosis became a permanent feature of **eukaryotic** cells.

A mitochondrion is the site of aerobic respiration.

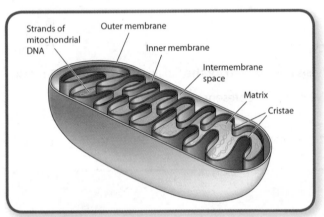

The structure of the mitochondrion is related to its function. Enclosing the mitochondrial contents is a plasma membrane, the outer membrane. The inner membrane has a number of folds that are called cristae. Between the outer and inner membranes is the intermembrane space. The matrix fills the innermost part of the mitochondrion. It contains the enzymes needed for respiration as well as mitochondrial DNA.

Outer Membrane
The outer membrane is a plasma membrane that contains protein channels called **porins** that allow small proteins to move into the mitochondrion. Molecules such as ATP, ADP, ions and nutrients can easily pass through this membrane.

Inner Membrane
The inner membrane is more restrictive than the outer membrane. It is feely permeable to oxygen, carbon dioxide and water. The structure of this membrane is more complex. It is a plasma membrane but with a number of protein structures incorporated, including ATP synthase, transport proteins and all the parts of the electron transport chain.

Cristae
The **cristae** massively increase the surface area of the inner membrane. This means that the number of transport proteins that it can hold is far higher than if the membrane were flat. It also increases the area available for diffusion.

Matrix
The matrix is a fluid filling the space between the cristae. It contains the enzymes that are involved in the Krebs cycle, as well as dissolved oxygen, water, carbon dioxide and the various intermediates for the different reactions.

Four Stages in Aerobic Respiration
Respiration can be divided into four stages, or steps, based on where the reactions for each step take place. The steps are glycolysis, which takes place in the cytoplasm of the cell, the link reaction, in the matrix, the Krebs cycle (or citric acid cycle), which also takes place in the matrix, and the electron transport chain, which takes place between the cristae and the intermembrane space.

Glycolysis
The first stage of respiration is the process of **glycolysis**. It is a catabolic process, which means that large molecules, such as glucose, are broken down into smaller ones.

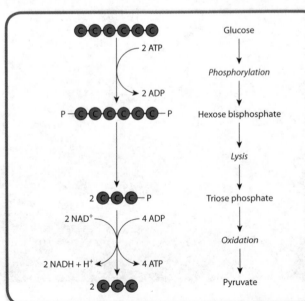

...e first step in glycolysis is for the six-carbon glucose ...olecule to be phosphorylated from the conversion ...two ATP molecules into two ADP molecules. This ...eates hexose bisphosphate. This molecule is broken ...sed) into two triose phosphate molecules.

...iose phosphate is then oxidised to form two ...olecules of pyruvate, via the conversion of four ...olecules of ADP into four molecules of ATP and ...wo molecules of NAD^+ being reduced to form two ...olecules each of NADH and H^+.

...his means that, although two molecules of ATP ...d to be used at the start of glycolysis, four ATP are ...ade at the end. Therefore, there are a total of two ATP ...d two NADH molecules produced overall through ...ycolysis.

...lycolysis does not involve mitochondria nor any ...xygen: it is therefore anaerobic.

The Link Reaction

...he **link reaction** takes the pyruvate formed through ...ycolysis and converts it into a molecule that feeds ...to the Krebs cycle (hence the term, *link* reaction). ...he pyruvate produced through glycolysis can pass ...rough the outer and inner membranes of the ...itochondrion into the matrix.

...he pyruvate is decarboxylated with coenzyme A (CoA) ...y the removal of CO_2 to form acetyl CoA. The equation ...s shown below.

$$\text{Pyruvate + CoA} \xrightarrow[\text{NAD}^+]{\text{NADH + H}^+} \text{acetyl CoA + CO}_2$$

...he process requires the reduction of NAD^+ to form ...ADH.

The Krebs Cycle

...he **Krebs cycle** converts acetyl CoA, the product of ...ne link reaction, into a number of different organic ...olecules.

...he first step is the formation of citrate from the ...eaction of oxaloacetate with acetyl CoA. The citrate ...s converted into other molecules, while producing ...wo CO_2 molecules from decarboxylation of two ...f the intermediate molecules and a total of three ...ADH molecules and one $FADH_2$ molecule from ...ne reduction of NAD^+ and FAD for every turn of ...ne cycle.

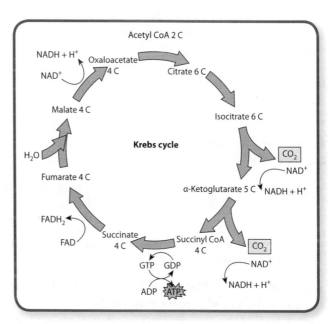

The site of the Krebs cycle is inside the matrix of the mitochondrion.

Oxidative Phosphorylation

The final stage of respiration is **oxidative phosphorylation** or the electron transport chain.

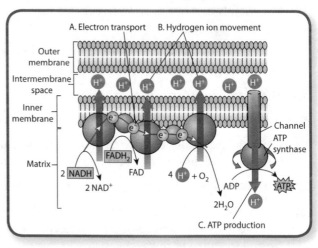

The electron transport chain is located on the inner membrane of the mitochondrion. A sequence of four protein complexes, along with **ATP synthase**, are embedded in the inner membrane.

Electrons are fed into complex I. NADH is converted into NAD^+ using NADH reductase and protons pumped into the intermembrane space. This increases the concentration of hydrogen ions in the intermembrane space. Complex II receives $FADH_2$, which also delivers electrons to the electron transport chain. Complex III accepts the electrons from complexes I and II and delivers them to complex IV. Complex IV reduces oxygen and the reduced oxygen then takes two hydrogen ions from the surrounding matrix to produce water.

The movement of electrons from one complex to another releases energy which allows protons to be moved against the proton concentration gradient.

The proton gradient caused by the increased proton concentration in the intermembrane space then drives ATP synthase to produce ATP.

The electron transport chain and ATP synthase are coupled together, which means they both have to be present to function.

SUMMARY

- Respiration is the process in which energy stored in complex molecules is transferred to ATP. The ATP is then used for metabolic processes.

- The mitochondrion is an organelle that used to be an endosymbiotic prokaryotic organism. It is the site of aerobic respiration.

- Enclosing the mitochondrion is the outer plasma membrane, which contains protein channels called porins that allow small proteins to enter. ATP, ADP, ions and nutrients all pass easily though the outer membrane.

- The inner membrane has many folds called cristae. The cristae increase the surface area of the inner membrane, which is feely permeable to water, O_2 and CO_2.

- The membrane has protein structures such as ATP synthase, transport proteins and all of the electron transport chain.

- The mitrochondrial matrix contains enzymes involved in the Krebs cycle (or citric acid cycle) as well as dissolved O_2, H_2O, CO_2 and the various intermediates for the reactions.

- There are four stages in aerobic respiration.

- Glycolysis is an anaerobic catabolic process taking place in the cell cytoplasm.

- Glucose undergoes a series of reactions, eventually producing the three-carbon pyruvate. Overall, two net molecules of ATP and two NAD^+ molecules are produced from glycolysis.

- The link reaction converts pyruvate to acetyl CoA by decarboxylation with coenzyme A (CoA).

- The Krebs cycle is a series of reactions taking place in the matrix, converting acetyl CoA into a series of organic molecules. Two molecules of CO_2 are produced, with three NADH and one $FADH_2$, from every turn of the cycle.

- Oxidative phosphorylation is the final stage of respiration. It is where electrons are fed into the electron transport chain.

- NADH and $FADH_2$ are converted to NAD^+ and FAD, and protons are pumped into the intermembrane space.

- The movement of protons back into the matrix is through ATP synthase, generating ATP.

1. Define respiration.

2. What organelle is the site of aerobic respiration?

3. Draw and label this organelle.

4. What molecules can pass easily through the outer membrane?

5. What is the function of cristae?

6. What does the matrix contain?

7. What are the four steps in aerobic respiration?

8. How many molecules of NADH, $FADH_2$ and CO_2 are produced for every turn of the Krebs cycle?

9. What is oxidative phosphorylation?

10. What molecule in the membrane generates ATP?

PRACTICE QUESTIONS

1.

Look at the diagram, which shows some of the reactions occurring in aerobic respiration.

a) i) Which stages of aerobic respiration do X, Y and Z represent? [3 marks]

   ii) Where does reaction Z occur? [1 mark]

   iii) One electron carrier has **not** been shown in the diagram. What is its name? [1 mark]

b) In reaction Y the pyruvate undergoes decarboxylation. What is meant by the term decarboxylation? [1 mark]

c) If the process stops before stage Y, what type of respiration would be taking place? [1 mark]

Holoenzymes

The reactions in the different stages of respiration are catalysed by enzymes. These lower the activation energy of the reactions, enabling them to take place faster and at low temperatures. Many enzymes, including those involved in cellular respiration, cannot function on their own. They need to combine with non-protein cofactors. The enzyme without the cofactor is called the **apoenzyme**. The complex that forms between apoenzyme and cofactor is called a **holoenzyme**.

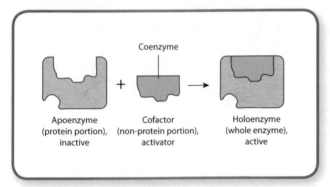

Apoenzyme (protein portion), inactive + Cofactor (non-protein portion), activator → Holoenzyme (whole enzyme), active

Coenzyme

The cofactor is a non-protein group that either is bound tightly to the enzyme or is a **coenzyme** that leaves the enzyme after the reaction has occurred.

Coenzymes

Coenzymes are not specific to a particular enzyme. They can be used and reused in a number of different chemical reactions. Unlike enzymes, they are changed in the chemical reaction and can therefore be regarded as being a substrate in a reaction.

The purpose of the coenzyme is to transport chemical groups between the different enzymes in a metabolic pathway.

NAD^+

The coenzyme **NAD^+** is one of the most important coenzymes in the cell. It is made from vitamin B_3. It accepts hydrogen atoms in oxidation/reduction reactions. Each NAD^+ can accept two electrons, but only one proton is attached to NAD^+; the other is released into the surrounding medium.

$$NAD^+ + 2H^+ + 2e^- \rightarrow NADH + H^+$$

NAD^+ is used in the reactions of glycolysis and the Krebs cycle. The hydrogen and electrons are passed to the next part of the metabolic pathway.

FAD

FAD is an electron carrier that is an important coenzyme in metabolic reactions. FAD is reduced to $FADH_2$ by the addition of two hydrogen atoms and two electrons.

$$FAD + 2H^+ + 2e^- \rightarrow FADH_2$$

$FADH_2$ releases the protons and electrons, passing them to the next part of the metabolic pathway.

Coenzyme A

Coenzyme A, or CoA, is one of the most active coenzymes in the body. It binds with pyruvate to form the two-carbon acetyl coenzyme A (acetyl CoA), which can be completely oxidised to CO_2 in the Krebs cycle. It is also the building block for fatty acids, cholesterol and other compounds.

Chemiosmotic Theory

The chemiosmotic theory describes how the electron transport chain works. The electron transport chain is the transfer of electrons down an electron transport system through a series of oxidation/reduction reactions, leading to the pumping of protons up a concentration gradient. The protons move back into the matrix down a concentration gradient through ATP synthase, which converts $ADP + P_i$ into ATP.

The electron transport chain and ATP synthase are found in mitochondria for respiration as well as in the chloroplast for photosynthesis, where it forms the basis of photophosphorylation.

Aerobic Respiration

The aerobic respiration of one molecule of glucose makes the products shown in the table at the top of the next page.

In practice, the amount of ATP produced is lower due to the energy required to move the substrates into the mitochondria. This means that 30–32 ATP is more normally produced from a single glucose molecule.

Process	ATP produced directly by substrate-level phosphorylation	Reduced coenzyme	ATP produced by oxidative phosphorylation	Total
Glycolysis	Net 2 ATP	2 NADH	4–6 ATP	6–8
Oxidation of pyruvate (link reaction)	—	2 NADH	6 ATP	6
Krebs cycle	2 ATP	6 NADH	18 ATP	24
		2 FADH$_2$	4 ATP	
			Total	36–38

Anaerobic Respiration

Anaerobic respiration takes place in the cytoplasm of the cell. The mitochondria, if present, are not involved.

Glycolysis is anaerobic. At the end of glycolysis the cell has to either continue the process aerobically or it must instead follow an anaerobic pathway.

The net ATP produced through glycolysis is two molecules of ATP, which can be used in metabolism. The two NADH molecules produced cannot be converted back to NAD$^+$ through oxidative phosphorylation. Instead they follow either a **homolactic** or alcoholic fermentation pathway, depending upon the nature of the cell. The total ATP produced is two ATP, which is far lower than is produced through the stages of aerobic respiration.

Homolactic Fermentation

In mammalian cells, anaerobic respiration involves the reaction of NADH with pyruvate in the presence of the enzyme lactate dehydrogenase to form lactate and NAD$^+$. The lactate is then converted into lactic acid.

$$Pyruvate + NADH \rightarrow NAD^+ + lactate$$

$$Lactate + H^+ \rightleftharpoons lactic\ acid$$

When muscles work at high intensity for a long time the body cannot supply enough oxygen for respiration to be aerobic. This is when anaerobic respiration occurs. The product, lactic acid, causes muscle cramps and fatigue.

Alcoholic Fermentation

In organisms such as yeast, anaerobic respiration progresses through alcoholic fermentation. The anaerobic conditions in yeast convert pyruvate into carbon dioxide and ethanol using the enzyme pyruvate decarboxylase. The reaction sequence involves carbon dioxide being removed from the pyruvate, leaving acetaldehyde.

$$Pyruvate \rightarrow acetaldehyde + carbon\ dioxide$$

The acetaldehyde is then reduced by the enzyme alcohol dehydrogenase, transferring hydrogen from NADH to the acetaldehyde, yielding NAD$^+$ and ethanol.

$$Acetaldehyde + NADH \rightarrow ethanol + NAD^+$$

This does not occur in mammals as they do not possess alcohol dehydrogenase.

Substrates for Respiration

Respiration does not only utilise glucose. Different substrates can be used to liberate energy. Carbohydrates, such as starch, are treated in the same way as glucose, having been broken down into monosaccharides first. The only monosaccharide that can be respired is glucose, but most of the other sugars can easily be converted into glucose when needed.

Lipids

Lipids can be used as a substrate for aerobic respiration. Lipids are stored in **adipose cells**. Lipids are broken down into glycerol and fatty acids in the liver by the process of lipolysis. The glycerol is easily converted into an intermediate of glycolysis. It then enters the aerobic respiration pathway. The fatty acids are converted into acetyl CoA molecules via beta-oxidation and then enter the Krebs cycle. Lipids therefore produce more energy compared to glucose.

Proteins

Proteins can be used as a substrate for aerobic respiration if the amount of protein available is high and glucose and fat sources are depleted. The amino acids making up the protein first have to be deaminated (the amino acid removed) or transaminated (the amine group transferred to another amino acid). This leads to molecules that can then feed directly into the Krebs cycle.

Respiratory Quotient

The **respiratory quotient (RQ)** is a measure of the ratio of carbon dioxide given out to the oxygen consumed by an organism over a given period of time.

$$RQ = \frac{CO_{2\ eliminated}}{O_{2\ consumed}}$$

The RQ can be used to work out the type of respiratory substrate being used. The RQ values for the following substrates have been determined.

Source	RQ value
Carbohydrate	1.0
Protein	0.9
Fat	0.7

If there is a mixture of substrates being used, then the ratio will have a different value, reflecting the mixture of substrates.

Measuring RQ

The device used to measure RQ is a respirometer.

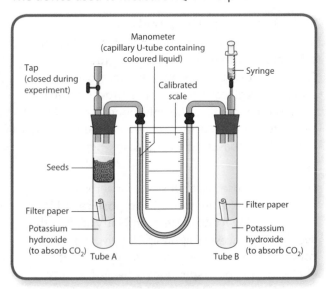

In the respirometer, potassium hydroxide is used to absorb the carbon dioxide in the apparatus. As the seeds germinate, they use oxygen, reducing the pressure in tube A. This draws the liquid in the manometer further up on the left hand side. Carbon dioxide produced through respiration is captured by the potassium hydroxide solution. The syringe in tube B is then used to remove a volume of gas to reset the manometer. The volume of gas withdrawn represents the amount of O_2 that has been used (noted as volume A). The experiment is run again with water instead of potassium hydroxide. The change in levels here represents the amount of CO_2 that has been expired (volume B). From this, the RQ value can be calculated.

$$RQ = \frac{Volume\ A - Volume\ B}{Volume\ A}$$

QUICK TEST

1. What do enzymes do to the activation energy for a reaction?

2. How do holoenzymes and apoenzymes differ from each other?

3. How do coenzymes differ from enzymes?

4. What is the role of a coenzyme?

5. Write the equation for the reduction of NAD^+.

6. What does coenzyme A bind with before entering the Krebs cycle?

7. Show how many ATP molecules are produced from the aerobic respiration of one molecule of glucose. Refer to each stage of respiration.

8. How many more times inefficient is anaerobic respiration compared to aerobic respiration?

9. Write the equations leading to the formation of lactic acid in mammals.

10. Why can't mammals ferment glucose to produce alcohol?

SUMMARY

- **Enzymes lower the activation energy of reactions, allowing them to take place at a lower temperature and a faster rate.**

- **Many enzymes have to combine with non-protein cofactors or coenzymes to work. The apoenzyme is the enzyme without its cofactor; the holoenzyme is the enzyme with its cofactor.**

- The cofactor is a non-protein group that either is tightly bound to the enzyme or is a coenzyme that leaves the enzyme after the reaction has occurred.

- Coenzymes are not specific to a particular enzyme; they can be reused in a number of different reactions. Unlike enzymes, they are changed in the reaction and therefore are regarded as being a substrate.

- Coenzymes transport chemical groups between the different enzymes in a metabolic pathway.

- NAD^+ is a coenzyme made from vitamin B_3. It is a hydrogen acceptor in oxidation/reduction reactions. FAD is a hydrogen and electron carrier reduced to $FADH_2$ by adding two hydrogen atoms and two electrons.

- Coenzyme A binds with pyruvate to form acetyl coenzyme A (acetyl CoA), which feeds into the Krebs cycle. It is also a building block for fatty acids, cholesterol and other organic compounds.

- Chemiosmotic theory describes how the electron transport chain works. The electron transport chain transfers electrons through oxidative phosphorylation.

- Ultimately protons are pumped through ATP synthase, converting ADP + P_i into ATP.

- The electron transport chain is present in mitochondria and chloroplasts.

- Aerobic respiration produces:
  - 6–8 ATP from glycolysis (2 ATP + the oxidative phosphorylation of 2 NADH)
  - 6 ATP from the oxidation of pyruvate (the oxidative phosphorylation of 2 NADH)
  - 24 ATP from the Krebs cycle (2 ATP + the oxidative phosphorylation of 6 NADH and 2 $FADH_2$).

- Anaerobic respiration takes place in the cytoplasm; mitochondria are not involved.

- The net ATP from the anaerobic respiration of one glucose molecule is 2 ATP.

- In mammals, pyruvate is converted into lactic acid (homolactic fermentation). In yeast, alcoholic fermentation occurs.

- Respiratory quotient (RQ) is the ratio of carbon dioxide given out to the oxygen consumed in a given period. It is used to determine the substrate(s) used for respiration.

PRACTICE QUESTIONS

1. If not enough oxygen is present for aerobic respiration, pyruvate builds up and is metabolised in other reactions. How is the pyruvate metabolised in mammalian cells? **[2 marks]**

2. An experiment was set up to measure the respiratory quotient (RQ) of seeds and seedlings at different stages of germination and growth. The table shows the results from the experiment.

Stage of germination and growth	RQ
Seeds soaked in water	1.0
Seeds after 12 hours in the soil	0.7
Seedlings after 25 days in the soil	1.0

a) What does RQ measure? **[1 mark]**

b) Explain the RQ values for each stage of germination and growth shown in the table. **[6 marks]**

Mutations

A large variety of different **metabolic reactions** take place in a cell. A specific cell type will carry out a subset of all the possible reactions. The control of the processes that take place inside the cell depends on which genes are switched on in that cell. The metabolic reactions undertaken by a specific cell determine the role of the cell and ultimately how the organism will grow, develop and function.

As discussed in *A Level in a Week Biology* Year 1, **mutations** are permanent changes in the genetic code. The entire sequence of proteins that derives from the genetic code is called the **proteome**. The changes have to take place in the gamete-producing cells for them to be inherited by offspring.

There are a number of different types of mutation:
- **substitution:** where a nucleotide gets swapped with another, incorrect, nucleotide
- **insertion:** where a new nucleotide or nucleotides are inserted into a DNA sequence
- **deletion:** where a nucleotide or nucleotides are deleted from a DNA sequence.

The effects of these mutations can be classed as being neutral, beneficial or harmful.

Neutral Mutations

A neutral mutation is one with which there is no difference to the function of the protein formed. In other words, there is no advantage or disadvantage. This is most likely to occur with a substitution mutation. To illustrate this, it is necessary to refer to the genetic code table (shown on the top right).

The table shows the mRNA bases that code for amino acids. There is **redundancy** built into the code (we can also say it is a degenerate code), with a number of alternative triplet codes coding for amino acids.

Taking the sequence:

…AUC AUC UUU GGU GUU UCC…

This codes for:

…Ile Ile Phe Gly Val Ser…

or:

…IIFGVS…

1st base	2nd base							3rd base

Standard genetic code

1st base	2nd base U		2nd base C		2nd base A		2nd base G		3rd base
U	UUU	(Phe/F) Phenylalanine	UCU	(Ser/S) Serine	UAU	(Tyr/Y) Tyrosine	UGU	(Cys/C) Cysteine	U
	UUC		UCC		UAC		UGC		C
	UUA	(Leu/L) Leucine	UCA		UAA	Stop	UGA	Stop	A
	UUG		UCG		UAG	Stop	UGG	(Trp/W) Tryptophan	G
C	CUU	(Leu/L) Leucine	CCU	(Pro/P) Proline	CAU	(His/H) Histidine	CGU	(Arg/R) Arginine	U
	CUC		CCC		CAC		CGC		C
	CUA		CCA		CAA	(Gln/Q) Glutamine	CGA		A
	CUG		CCG		CAG		CGG		G
A	AUU	(Ile/I) Isoleucine	ACU	(Thr/T) Threonine	AAU	(Asn/N) Asparagine	AGU	(Ser/S) Serine	U
	AUC		ACC		AAC		AGC		C
	AUA		ACA		AAA	(Lys/K) Lysine	AGA	(Arg/R) Arginine	A
	AUG	(Met/M) Methionine or start	ACG		AAG		AGG		G
G	GUU	(Val/V) Valine	GCU	(Ala/A) Alanine	GAU	(Asp/D) Aspartic acid	GGU	(Gly/G) Glycine	U
	GUC		GCC		GAC		GGC		C
	GUA		GCA		GAA	(Glu/E) Glutamic acid	GGA		A
	GUG		GCG		GAG		GGG		G

If there is a mutation in the third of these triplets:

…AUC AUC UUC GGU GUU UCC…

This also codes for:

…Ile Ile Phe Gly Val Ser…

or:

…IIFGVS…

UUC is a different codon but due to redundancy in the code the amino acid produced is still phenylalanine, Phe or F. The protein would function in exactly the same way as normal. If this occurred in the gamete-producing cells all offspring would carry this mutation.

It is possible for insertions and deletions to lead to neutral mutations, if the insertion or deletion is a multiple of three. Of course, the more bases inserted or deleted the greater the chance that such an event will have a significant effect on the function of the resulting protein.

Beneficial Mutations

A beneficial mutation occurs when the insertion, deletion or substitution leads to a protein that does a better job than the previous version or confers another benefit that was previously absent.

An example is a mutation that occurred to a protein involved in reducing the amount of cholesterol in the blood. The protein is called apolipoprotein A1, or Apo1. In the fourteenth century an individual was born who had an insertion of three nucleotides that coded for cysteine (Cys/C). This meant that an extra link (a cysteine bridge) is made in the quaternary structure, enabling Apo1 to join to another Apo1 unit, forming a homodimer. This mutation enables the individual carrying it to have a much reduced risk of heart disease and **atherosclerosis**. More carriers live to 100 years or more than those who carry the 'normal' version of the protein.

There are numerous other examples of longer survival caused by certain mutations. Mutations leading to the duplication of a gene can lead to new benefits. Taste receptors in humans are the result of numerous mutations. Some genes for taste receptors were copied and then mutations enabled them to detect different tastes.

Below is a phylogenetic tree showing how gene duplication led to the evolution in different species of receptors that detect a variety of tastes.

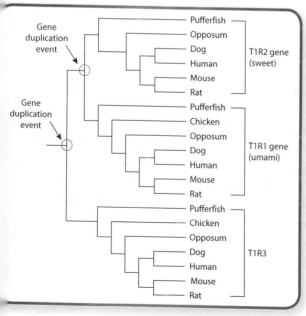

Harmful Mutations

There are a range of ways through with mutations can be harmful. The most obvious harmful mutation is one where the mutation takes place in such a vital protein that development of an embryo halts completely. For example, a mutation in the gene coding for coenzyme A could render it useless and the cell carrying it would not be able to respire aerobically.

Deletions, substitutions and insertions can lead to small, but significant changes in the function of an enzyme. For example, taking the earlier sequence:

…AUC AUC UUU GGU GUU UCC…

This codes for:

…Ile Ile Phe Gly Val Ser…

If there is a deletion of three nucleotides CUU then the sequence becomes:

…AUC AUU GGU GUU UCC…

This also codes for:

…Ile Ile Gly Val Ser…

This is because of redundancy. Isoleucine, I, is coded for by a number of different nucleotide sequences. It happens that AUU also codes for isoleucine and the remaining amino acids are also unaffected by the deletion.

This deletion could have had a neutral effect, but the removal of phenylalanine, F, causes a protein responsible for the transport of ions across the plasma membrane to work less effectively. A person with this mutation on both chromosomes will have cystic fibrosis.

Most metabolic reactions in the body involve a series of enzyme-controlled reactions. A mutation that slows down a reaction or stops it from working completely will affect an individual in different ways according to where the metabolic pathway has been broken or altered.

Phenylketonuria

Phenylalanine is an essential amino acid. There is a metabolic pathway that converts phenylalanine to tyrosine (another amino acid) and into a number of other metabolites, ultimately leading to acetoacetate.

The conversion of tyrosine into other metabolites is important. Tyrosinema II affects the skin, ears and mental development. Type III which involves a mutation in the enzyme further along the pathway is more severe with sufferers having intellectual disability, seizures and loss of balance and coordination. Type I is the most severe form with sufferers dying young, before the age of 10.

Harmful mutations therefore can have a range of harm. The harm is also viewed from a perspective of 'healthy' individuals. Although the gene mutation causing the most prevalent form of cystic fibrosis is 'harmful' to the individual it does confer an advantage conferring to carriers some protection against disease such as cholera and typhoid. Deciding whether a mutation is harmful can therefore be difficult.

SUMMARY

- Of all the possible metabolic reactions that can be undertaken by an organism, a cell will carry out a small subset of those reactions.
- Control of the processes inside a cell depends on which genes are switched on and off.
- Mutations are permanent changes in the genetic code that are passed onto offspring. Types of mutation include substitution, insertion and deletion.
- Mutations can be classed as being neutral, beneficial or harmful.
- Neutral mutations make a difference to the function of the protein formed. This is most likely to occur with substitution mutations.
- Redundancy in the genetic code helps to minimise the effect of substitution mutations.
- Amino acids such as proline (Pro, or P) can be coded for by six combinations of three bases. For instance, CCU, CCC, CCA and CCG all code for proline. Substituting the last nucleotide for any other has no effect on proline.
- If the substitution occurred in the first or second nucleotide, then it is more likely a new amino acid would be produced.
- Beneficial mutations occur when the insertion, deletion or substitution leads to a protein that does a better job than the previous protein or confers another benefit that was previously absent.
- Apolipoprotein A1 is a protein that is involved in reducing cholesterol. One mutation has an insertion of three nucleotides coding for cysteine (Cys, C), allowing Apo1 homodimers to form. This leads to a much reduced risk of heart disease and atherosclerosis compared with those who do not have the mutation.
- Harmful mutations occur when the mutation leads to a protein that does not function as well as the 'normal' version or it leads to the failure of the organism to develop at all.
- Most metabolic reactions are controlled by sequences of enzyme-controlled reactions. The earlier in the metabolic sequence the mutation occurs, the more likely it is that consequences will be severe.
- Phenylketonuria is a condition where a mutation affects the conversion of phenylalanine to tyrosine. Any of the enzymes along the phenylalanine to tyrosine pathway could be mutated, leading to a number of different metabolites being produced, some more dangerous than others.
- Tyrosinema II affects the skin, ears and mental development; type III is more severe and leads to intellectual disability, loss of balance and coordination.

1. What is an insertion mutation?

2. What is a substitution mutation?

3. What is a deletion mutation?

4. How can mutations be classed in terms of their effect?

5. How is it possible for a mutation to occur yet the polypeptide formed is unaffected?

6. Where in the triplet would a nucleotide substitution have the most impact on the amino acid produced?

7. What would need to happen to make a mutation beneficial?

8. Why do mutations have the potential to have a big impact on metabolism?

9. Two cells have a mutation, one at the start of the metabolic pathway and the other at the end. Which cell is more likely to be adversely affected?

10. Suggest why some mutations exist in a population even though they may cause harm.

PRACTICE QUESTIONS

1. The umami taste receptor, T1R1, enables the detection of savoury flavours, such as those found in meat.

The giant panda acquired two mutations in the T1R1 receptor. Sections of the gene encoding the taste receptor T1R1 are shown below.

Normal section A (in dogs)

DNA base sequence	TCA	TCA	GGT	CCA	GAA
Amino acid sequence	Ser, S	Ser, S	Pro, P	Gly, G	Leu, L

Section A in panda

DNA base sequence	TCA	TCA	GGT	CCG	GGA
Amino acid sequence	Ser, S	Ser, S	Pro, P	Gly, G	Pro, P

Normal section B (in dogs)

DNA base sequence	GTA	GTG	TAA	CCA	CCA
Amino acid sequence	His, H	Leu, L	Iso, I	Gly, G	Gly, G

Section B in panda

DNA base sequence	GTA	AAC	CAC	CAA
Amino acid sequence	Ser, S	Leu, L	Val, V	Val, V

a) What type of mutation has occurred in section A of the panda T1R1 gene? [2 marks]

b) What type of mutation has occurred in section B of the panda T1R1 gene? [2 marks]

c) What effect would the mutation have on the T1R1 protein? [3 marks]

d) Suggest a genetic reason as a possible explanation for why pandas eat bamboo and not meat. [2 marks]

Regulatory Mechanisms

Gene expression is controlled at three stages:
- **transcriptional** level
- **post-transcriptional** level
- **post-translational** level.

Transcriptional Level

Transcription takes place in the nucleus. It is the reading of the nucleotide sequence of a gene and conversion into mRNA that can leave the nucleus. At the transcriptional level the simplest way to control gene transcription is through **operons**.

Operons

An operon is a unit of DNA containing a cluster of genes that are controlled by a single **promoter**.

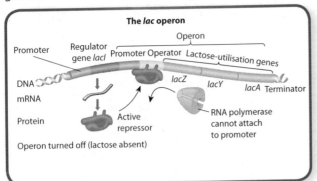

The lac operon

Operon turned off (lactose absent)

A regulator gene is transcribed into mRNA when it receives a signal that the genes under the control of the operon are not needed. The mRNA leads to the synthesis of a **repressor protein** which attaches to the **operator** section of the operon. When the repressor is bound to the operator, transcription cannot take place, so the genes that follow will not be transcribed.

An example is the *lac* operon in bacteria. It would be pointless producing enzymes to break down lactose if there were no lactose present. So, in the absence of lactose the regulator gene, *lacI*, produces a repressor protein that binds to the operator of the *lac* operon. Once in place, RNA polymerase fails to read the DNA so the genes for lactose utilisation are switched off. *lacZ* codes for β-galactosidase, which breaks the lactose into glucose and galactose; *lacY* encodes the enzyme lactose permease, which incorporates into the cell surface membrane to allow the transport of lactose into the cell; and *lacA* codes for galactoside-

O-acetyltransferase, which is involved in transferring acetyl coenzyme A to β-galactosidase, to prevent toxic build up of metabolites in the cell.

All three genes are controlled by the same regulator protein, produced by *lacI*.

Operons were previously thought to occur only in prokaryotes; however, in the 1990s a number of operons in eukaryotes were discovered, suggesting that they are more common than expected.

Transcription Factors

Eukaryotes are more complex than prokaryotes, but the number of genes present in each is not hugely different. The control of gene transcription is through **transcription factors**, which enable a larger number of proteins to be produced from a gene sequence. It is the transcription factors that switch genes on or off.

Transcription factors are proteins that bind to specific DNA sequences and control the rate of transcription from DNA to mRNA. Transcription factors can work on their own or as a complex with other proteins to promote the attaching or the blocking of RNA polymerase.

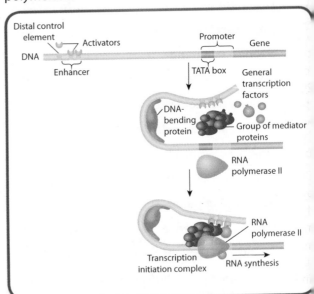

The steroid hormone oestrogen can switch on a gene and start transcription. Oestrogen binds to an oestrogen receptor on a transcription factor.

The transcription factor changes shape, releases an inhibitor molecule and can then bind to DNA, starting transcription.

Upstream of the gene sequence to be transcribed, enhancers are activated by activators. DNA is bent so that the enhancer region can interact with the mediator proteins and transcription factors. This allows a transcription initiation complex to form, enabling RNA polymerase to transcribe the relevant gene.

Post-transcriptional Level

In eukaryotes, a gene is comprised of **exons** and **introns**. The exons code for protein, whereas the introns do not. The pre-mRNA that is produced during transcription is edited by removal of the introns.

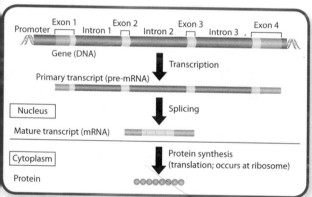

It is possible for the combination of exons and introns to be altered. This can mean that one gene can lead to a variety of different proteins to be formed. This is called alternative or differential splicing and accounts for how humans produce far more proteins than the 20 000 genes present in the genome. The splicing of the introns is controlled by ***trans*-acting proteins**, which act as repressors or activators.

Post-translational Level

Once the mRNA has left the nucleus it is translated by ribosomes. The polypeptide chain that forms can then be altered by other enzymes. Post-translational modification leads to the formation of the final, mature protein product. Different prosthetic groups, such as phosphate, acetate, methyl groups and amide groups can be covalently joined to the protein. Eukaryotes can have carbohydrate molecules attached through a process called glycosylation. Lipids can also be attached. Many of the modified proteins are used in cell signalling.

Epigenetics

Epigenetics is the study of the changes in organisms that are caused by the modification of gene expression rather than changing the DNA sequence itself. Changes in the environment have an effect on transcription, either enabling transcription or turning a gene off.

DNA Methylation

DNA methylation is where methyl groups are added to DNA. The only bases that can be methylated are cytosine and adenine. Adenine methylation only occurs in prokaryotes.

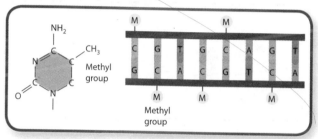

Methylation alters DNA function, typically repressing transcription. DNA methylation occurs naturally during development, including in embryo development and aging.

Histone Acetylation

Histones are eukaryotic proteins that package DNA into nucleosomes. When a histone is acetylated by the addition of acetyl CoA, the gene is transcribed. When the histones are deacetylated, transcription is stopped.

RNA Interference (RNAi)

In eukaryotes and some prokaryotes, RNA interference (RNAi) can occur, whereby RNA molecules inhibit gene expression, typically by causing the destruction of specific mRNA molecules from target genes.

Cancer

Benign tumours are non-cancerous and rarely cause serious problems or life-threatening conditions. They stay in one place and grow slowly. If removed surgically, they rarely recur. Malignant tumours are cancerous and vary in size and shape. The cells in the tumour divide uncontrollably in abnormal ways, invading other tissues, blood vessels or the lymph system. When they interfere with the function of the body, malign tumours become life-threatening. Some malignant cancer cells can break away from the primary tumour and travel to other parts of the body, causing new secondary tumours to form. This is called metastasis.

Genetic Control

Most cells have the potential for apoptosis (programmed cell death; see the next section). Oncogenes are genes that can make a cell cancerous. An oncogene has the potential to stop cells that should undergo apoptosis and cause them to proliferate instead. Normal genes can become oncogenes through mutation or abnormal expression. To respond to oncogenes, the genome includes tumour suppressor genes. These are genes that protect the cell by preventing cell proliferation through mitosis and inhibiting tumour development.

Abnormal methylation of oncogenes and tumour suppressor genes can lead to cancer. With some types of breast cancer there is an increase in the amount of the steroid hormone oestrogen. As seen, oestrogen can bind to transcription factors to initiate transcription.

By understanding the genetics and epigenetics of gene expression scientists can develop new ways to treat, prevent and potentially cure cancer.

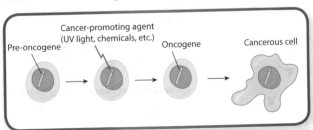

SUMMARY

- Gene expression is controlled at three stages: transcription, post-transcription, post-translation.
- Transcription in the nucleus is controlled via operons. An operon is a unit of DNA containing a cluster of genes controlled by a single promoter.
- A regulator gene is transcribed into mRNA when it receives a signal that the genes under the control of the operon are not needed.
- The mRNA leads to the synthesis of a repressor protein that attaches to the operator section of the operon. When the repressor is bound to the operator, transcription cannot take place.
- The *lac* operon in prokaryotes is an example of an operon. When lactose is not present the regulator gene *lacI* produces a repressor which attaches to the operator of the *lac* operon.
- RNA polymerase fails to read the DNA, so the lactose-utilisation genes are switched off.
- Eukaryotes are more complex than prokaryotes, yet have fewer genes than would be expected. Control of genes in eukaryotes is through transcription factors, enabling a larger number of proteins to be made from a gene sequence.
- Transcription factors are proteins that bind to specific DNA sequences, controlling the rate of transcription. They work on their own or as a complex with other proteins.
- An example is the steroid hormone oestrogen, which binds to its transcription factor.
- This changes the shape of the transcription factor, causing it to bind DNA and transcription to start.
- Enhancers are activated by activators upstream of the gene sequence being transcribed.
- DNA is bent so that the enhancer region can interact with mediator proteins and transcription factors. This allows a transcription initiation complex to form, allowing RNA polymerase to transcribe the gene.

- Eukaryotic genes are comprised of exons, which code for protein, and introns, which do not. Different versions of proteins are produced by altering which exons and introns are removed.

- Post-translational modification involves other prosthetic groups being added to the protein. These groups alter the properties of the protein.

- Epigenetics is the study of the changes caused by the modification of gene expression rather than changing the DNA sequence itself.

- Examples include methylation of DNA and the action of histone proteins.

- RNAi can effectively destroy mRNA sequences.

- Oncogenes can make a cell cancerous whereas tumour suppressing cells prevent mitosis of cancer cells.

QUICK TEST

1. What is an operon?

2. When is a regulator gene transcribed?

3. What protein is transcribed by the regulator gene?

4. How does the protein in question 3 affect the operon?

5. In bacteria, when is the *lacI* operon functional?

6. Eukaryotes are more complex than prokaryotes yet have approximately the same number of genes. How is this possible?

7. What is a transcription factor?

8. What are exons and introns?

9. How does pre-mRNA differ from mRNA?

10. What happens in post-translational modification?

PRACTICE QUESTIONS

1. Many bacteria are able to break down the disaccharide lactose into galactose and glucose. Lactose metabolism is governed at the transcriptional level by an operon. The diagram below shows an operon.

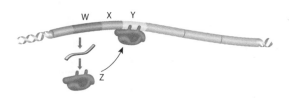

a) Identify the parts of the operon labelled W, X and Y. [3 marks]

b) Under what circumstance would Z be produced? [1 mark]

c) Using the diagram, explain how the operon functions when lactose is absent. [4 marks]

Embryonic Development

The instructions in the chromosomes code for the structure of the organism. The genes that control body structures in embryonic development of animals are similar to those found in plants and fungi, pointing to a common ancestor. The genes that control body plans are called **homeobox gene sequences**.

Homeobox Gene Sequences

Homeobox gene sequences are a large family of master developmental control genes regulating cell differentiation and the development of anatomical body structures. A **homeobox gene** is around 180 base pairs long and encodes a homeodomain protein comprised of about 60 amino acids. Homeodomain proteins are transcription factors. The proteins produced have sites to which DNA can bind.

> **Example**
> RRRKRTA-YTRYQLLE-LEKEFLF-
> NRYLTRRRRIELAHSL-
> NLTERHIKIWFQNRRMKWKKEN

In the amino acid sequence above, the dashes indicate where the DNA binds.

The homeobox initiates the transcription of relevant genes coding for the tissues and organs of the organism. Once initiated, this leads to a cascade of other transcription factors being initiated. It is a little like the boot-up sequence of a computer. The homeobox genes start the process. If these genes do not work, then there won't be an organism.

In humans there are approximately 235 functional genes that form the homeobox, along with around 65 genes that are structurally similar but do not provide instructions for making proteins.

Hox Genes

The **Hox** genes are the homeobox genes concerned with the development of **embryonic** regions from head to tail. The position of the Hox genes on the chromosome corresponds to the order the organs appear on the body, with genes active in the head coming first and the tail last, as indicated by the colours on the next figure.

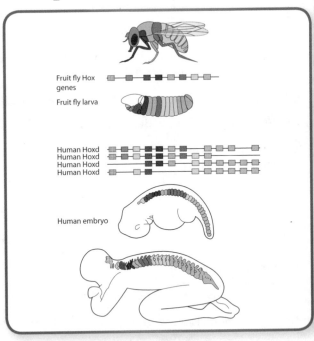

Fruit fly Hox genes

Fruit fly larva

Human Hoxd
Human Hoxd
Human Hoxd
Human Hoxd

Human embryo

The Hox genes are highly conserved in organisms. This means that the nucleotides that make up the Hox sequence do not vary greatly between organisms and only minor changes have occurred over hundreds of millions of years. This is because mutations would easily disrupt the function of the homeobox and probably be lethal. The Hox gene is evidence for a common ancestor of all animals.

Mitosis and Apoptosis

Cells spend 95% of their existence in the **interphase** before going through mitosis.

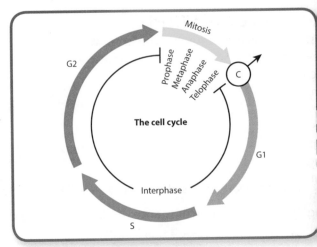

Mitosis

G2

Prophase
Metaphase
Anaphase
Telophase

C

The cell cycle

G1

S

Interphase

Mitosis is the process of cell division so new cells are made. **Apoptosis** is programmed cell death in multicellular organisms and leads to a reduction of cells. In an average human adult, around 50–70 billion cells die each day through apoptosis. The development of a new organism relies on mitosis to build up the number of cells and apoptosis to develop the form of the organism.

Apoptosis

Once apoptosis has been initiated, it is very difficult to stop so the process is highly regulated. The entire process must be contained within the targeted cell, otherwise the enzymes involved could break down other cells. Cells contain genes that code for **proteases**. When a signal to initiate apoptosis is received, proteases are released and a sequence of events occurs to remove the cell. Once the cell contents have been broken down, the cell is phagocytosed by macrophages.

There are two pathways leading to apoptosis: **extrinsic** and **intrinsic**. Both pathways lead to the production of initiator proteases that then activate executioner proteases, which break down all proteins in the cell.

Extrinsic Pathway

The extrinsic pathway is followed when the signal for apoptosis is received from other cells. It is followed in embryo development. During the development of an embryo there are a number of transitory organs and tissues. These are produced because the organism contains the historical gene sequences for those organs and tissues, but they are not needed in the organism. This includes organs such as the pronephros, which is a very basic excretory organ that develops early on during the first stage of kidney development in vertebrates.

Tissue remodelling enables the structure of the tissue or organ to be altered after it has formed. Development of the digits in the limb is an example. Apoptosis is essential to separate the fingers in the human hand. If it fails then the fingers can be webbed.

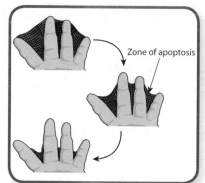
Zone of apoptosis

Intrinsic Pathway

The intrinsic pathway of apoptosis is initiated by intracellular signals generated when cells are stressed. Mitochondria are essential to all multicellular life. When the cell is under stress, genes are activated that cause mitochondrial proteins to be released from the intermembrane space of mitochondria. The mitochondrial proteins bind to protein inhibitors of apoptosis. As the inhibitors are not inactive, the release occurs of the proteases that then break down the cell.

Variation

The features of the body of an organism are coded for by the genes that are switched on. The observable characteristics an organism possesses are described by the phenotype. The phenotype of any characteristic is based on both genetic and environmental factors. Environmental factors, such as diet, amount of light, etc., can combine with genetic factors to produce the phenotype. For example, plants will grow towards a light source. The light source is the environmental factor and the genetic factor is the genes that encode the auxin plant growth regulator system.

SUMMARY

● Genes controlling body structures in the embryonic development of animals are similar to those found in plants and fungi, pointing to evolution from a common ancestor.

● Homeobox sequences control genes regulating cell differentiation and the development of the anatomy.

● A typical homeobox gene sequence is around 180 base pairs long and encodes a homeodomain protein of 60 amino acids.

● Homeodomain proteins are transcription factors with sites for DNA binding.

● The homeobox initiates transcription of the relevant genes coding for tissues and organs. This leads to a cascade of other transcription factors being initiated. If the homeobox fails to work, the organism will not develop.

● There are around 235 functional genes forming the homeobox of a human, along with 65 genes that are similar in structure but do not provide instructions for making protein.

● Hox genes are the homebox genes concerned with the development of embryonic regions from head to tail.

● The position of each Hox gene on the chromosome corresponds to the order in which the organs appear in the body.

● The Hox genes for the head appear first, those for the organs in the thorax next and those at the tail end of the organism last.

● Hox genes are highly conserved, varying only slightly over millions of years, which is evidence of a common ancestor.

● Growth of an organism is through mitosis.

● Apoptosis is the controlled death of cells; each day 50–70 billion cells die in an adult human.

● Apoptosis is highly regulated to ensure that only the target cell dies.

● During embryonic development there are a number of transitory tissues and organs, which arise from historical gene sequences that are no longer needed.

● The pronephros is a basic excretory organ that develops as part of kidney development in vertebrates.

● Tissue remodelling enables the structure of a tissue or organ to be altered after it has been formed.

● The webbing between human fingers is removed through apoptosis.

● Embryonic apoptosis follows the extrinsic pathway where the signals are received from other cells.

● The intrinsic pathway is followed when cells become stressed.

● Genes are activated that cause mitochondrial proteins to be released from the intermembrane space.

● The mitochondrial proteins bind to the protein inhibitors for apoptosis. This leads to proteases being released that break down the cell.

● The observable features of an organism are described by the phenotype.

● The phenotype results from a combination of genetic and environmental factors.

1. How do the genes of animal embryonic development point to a common ancestor?

2. What to homeobox gene sequences control?

3. What type of proteins are encoded by homeobox gene sequences?

4. What happens if the homeobox genes are faulty?

5. In humans, how many homeobox sequences are there?

6. What are Hox genes?

7. Why is the position where the Hox genes appear on the chromosome important?

8. What is apoptosis?

9. Why is apoptosis highly regulated?

10. What organelle is involved in the intrinsic pathway of apoptosis?

PRACTICE QUESTIONS

The homeobox gene sequences are very similar in an enormous range of animals. Investigating genes in *Drosophila*, scientists were able to transform the insect, creating flies that had feet in place of their mouth parts, and extra pairs of wings. Some even had legs growing in place of the antennae.

Normal fruit fly

Fruit fly with mutation in the antennapedia gene

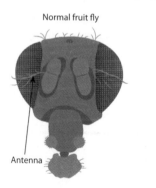
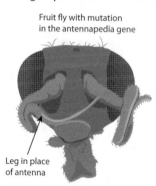

Antenna

Leg in place of antenna

These modifications were called homeotic transformations.

a) What does the fact that an antennal cell could develop into a leg tell you about the genetic information carried in every cell? **[1 mark]**

b) What is meant by the term homeobox gene? **[2 marks]**

c) The homeobox genes have been found in most animals. They have also been found in other kingdoms. Name another kingdom that has similar homeotic genes. **[1 mark]**

d) Why are the homeobox genes so highly conserved? **[2 marks]**

e) What do homeobox genes tell us about evolution? **[1 mark]**

Inheritance

Monogenic Inheritance

A condition that is caused by a problem with a single gene is passed on by **monogenic** (or monohybrid) **inheritance**.

Humans are **diploid** and so carry two copies of every chromosome. For every gene there are two copies, which means that there can be two different alleles. The word allele means version of a gene.

Monogenic inheritance can be shown using **Punnett squares**. In a condition where there are two possible alleles, an individual can be homozygous dominant, homozygous recessive or heterozygous dominant for a condition. Below, for the genetic disorder cystic fibrosis, F represents the dominant allele and f is the recessive allele.

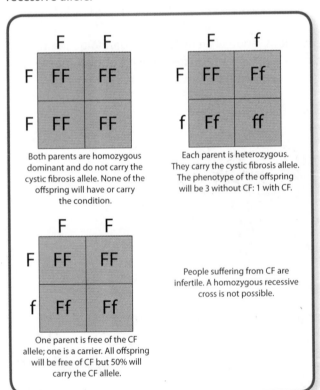

Both parents are homozygous dominant and do not carry the cystic fibrosis allele. None of the offspring will have or carry the condition.

Each parent is heterozygous. They carry the cystic fibrosis allele. The phenotype of the offspring will be 3 without CF: 1 with CF.

People suffering from CF are infertile. A homozygous recessive cross is not possible.

One parent is free of the CF allele; one is a carrier. All offspring will be free of CF but 50% will carry the CF allele.

A monogenic condition can also be represented using a family tree or pedigree chart. The next figure shows a cystic fibrosis pedigree. Roman numerals indicate the generation and the numbers 1, 2, 3 etc. identify the person. I-1 and I-2 are carriers for CF and II-3 has the condition.

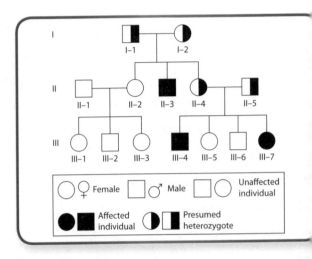

Dihybrid Inheritance

Many characteristics are controlled by two genes. **Dihybrid inheritance** is where a condition is controlled by two genes that are not linked; in other words, each allele has an equal chance of being present in a gamete. Each contributing gene has two alleles, which are represented in the same way as for monogenic crosses i.e. with a capital letter for the dominant allele and a lower-case letter for the recessive trait.

Once again, Punnett squares are used to predict the possible offspring. Peas can be yellow (Y, dominant) or green (y, recessive) and round (R, dominant) or wrinkled (r, recessive).

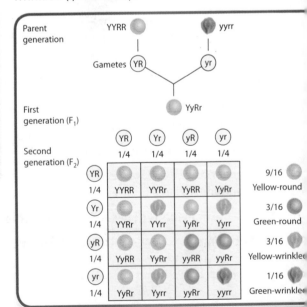

Multiple Alleles

In the cases presented so far, there have been only two alleles for a condition. It is easily possible to have more than two versions of a gene. If there are more than three phenotypes for a given trait, then there must be more than two alleles for that trait in a population.

An example is blood group in humans.

The gene for blood group has three alleles, I^A for A group, I^B for B group and i for O group (sometimes O is also denoted I^O). The possible genotypes are therefore:

Genotype	Phenotype
$I^A I^A$	Group A
$I^A i$	Group A
$I^B I^B$	Group B
$I^B i$	Group B
$I^A I^B$	Group AB
ii	Group O

There are six genotypes and four phenotypes. A and B are dominant to O. With group AB, both alleles are expressed, rather than one or the other being dominant. This is called **codominance**.

Codominance

Codominance occurs when neither of a pair of alleles is dominant to the other. This means that both alleles are expressed, leading to a third phenotype.

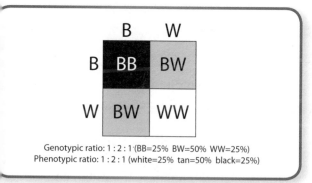

Genotypic ratio: 1 : 2 : 1 (BB=25% BW=50% WW=25%)
Phenotypic ratio: 1 : 2 : 1 (white=25% tan=50% black=25%)

Epistasis

Epistasis is where the expression of a gene is dependent upon the expression of a separate, modifier gene. For example, in pea plants two genes are responsible for the chemical reaction that produces the plant pigment anthocyanin from a precursor molecule:

Precursor molecule $\xrightarrow{A}$ Step 1 $\xrightarrow{B}$ Step 2 → anthocyanin

Gene A controls the first step in the reaction to produce the step 1 product. Gene B controls the second step in the reaction, leading to the production of anthocyanin. There are lots of genes that are reliant on epistasis for expression.

Sex Linkage

When an allele is dependent on the gender of the individual and is directly linked to the sex chromosomes (**allosome**) it is termed **sex linkage**.

In humans, as only males have a Y chromosome, any alleles on the Y chromosome can only be passed to male offspring. If an allele is present on the X chromosome, then either females or males can inherit the trait. Examples include colour blindness, some forms of haemophilia and Duchenne muscular dystrophy.

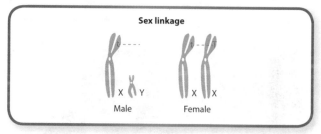

Sex linkage

X Y
Male

X X
Female

Female

	X^T	X^t
X^T	$X^T X^T$	$X^T X^t$
Y	$X^T Y$	$X^t Y$

Male

If a female is a carrier of a disorder, t, her sons have a 50% chance of having the condition. Her daughters will not have the condition, but may carry it.

Female

	X^T	X^T
X^t	$X^T X^t$	$X^T X^t$
Y	$X^T Y$	$X^T Y$

Male

If a male has an X-linked recessive allele and his partner is homozygous dominant, then all daughters will be carriers. No sons will carry or have the condition as the father does not contribute the X chromosome.

DAY 5

Sex linkage can be observed in pedigree charts. In the British royal family, Queen Victoria famously carried the gene for haemophilia, which is present on the X chromosome.

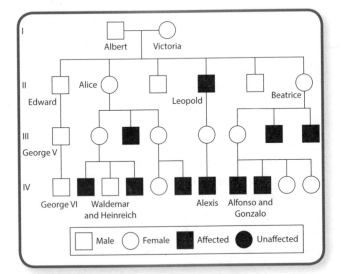

SUMMARY

- A condition that is caused by a single gene is passed on by monogenic inheritance.

- Humans are diploid, carrying two copies of each chromosome. For every gene there are two copies and therefore two alleles, which may differ.

- Monogenic inheritance can be shown using Punnett squares.

- With a gene where there are two possible alleles, with one allele dominant to the other, an individual can be homozygous dominant, e.g. TT, homozygous recessive, e.g. tt, or heterozygous dominant, e.g. Tt.

- Inheritance can also be represented through a family tree pedigree chart.

- Many characteristics are coded for by two genes. Dihybrid inheritance is where a condition is coded for by two genes that are not linked and not on the same chromosome.

- Each allele has an equal chance of being present in a gamete. Each contributing gene has two alleles that are represented in the same way as in monogenic crosses.

- It is possible to have more than two alleles for a gene. If there are more than four phenotypes for a trait then there must be more than two alleles for that trait.

- The gene for blood group has three alleles: I^A, I^B and i. This gives group A ($I^A I^A$ and I^Ai), group B ($I^B I^B$ and I^Bi), group AB ($I^A I^B$) and group O (ii). A and B groups are codominant.

- Codominance is where neither of a pair of alleles is dominant to the other so both are expressed, giving a third phenotype.

- Sex linkage is where an allele is dependent upon the gender of an individual and is directly linked to the sex chromosomes. If a condition is present on the Y chromosome, only males will express the condition. If an allele is present on the X chromosomes, both males and females will carry the trait.

- If the condition is recessive then males are more likely to get the condition as they will lack another X chromosome that could be dominant to it.

- If the male carries the recessive condition then all females born would carry it, but none of the males will (if the mother is homozygous dominant).

PRACTICE QUESTIONS

1. Rickets is a condition that most commonly results from vitamin D deficiency. It is also possible to have a mutation that interferes with the function of vitamin D. A sufferer will have rickets even if they receive enough sunlight or vitamin D in the diet.

A single gene controls vitamin D-resistant rickets. The gene is carried on the X chromosome. Its dominant allele causes vitamin D to be ineffective. A pedigree chart is shown below for a family with the condition.

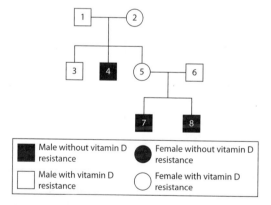

Male without vitamin D resistance
Female without vitamin D resistance
Male with vitamin D resistance
Female with vitamin D resistance

a) Explain, using the diagram, that lack of vitamin D resistance is caused by a recessive allele. **[2 marks]**

b) Explain, using the diagram, that vitamin D-resistant rickets is caused by a gene on the X chromosome. **[1 mark]**

c) What is the probability of the next child born to parents 5 and 6 not having vitamin D-resistant rickets? Use a Punnett square to illustrate your answer. **[4 marks]**

Variation

Continuous Variation

Continuous variation refers to variation where there is no limit on the value for a characteristic within the population. Continuous variation is caused by the interaction of many genes, along with environmental factors. This means that continuous variation is more difficult to research than **discontinuous variation** (see below).

Examples include weight and height. Graphs can be plotted to show the complete range of values for a trait.

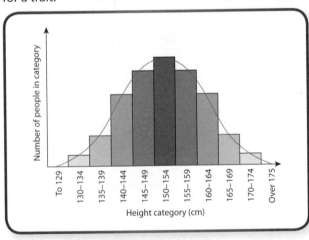

To make the data easy to read the data have been arranged in ranges and bars plotted as a histogram. When the sample size is large enough it is possible to see a normal distribution curve.

Discontinuous Variation

When a characteristic is coded for by one or two genes and is not affected by the environment, the trait will fit into distinct categories. This is discontinuous variation.

Examples include the ability to roll the tongue, blood group and 'hitchhiker's thumb'.

Data showing discontinuous variation is plotted as a bar chart. Unlike a histogram there are gaps between the bars. The bars can be plotted in any order.

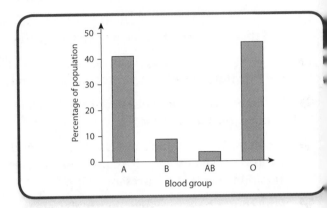

Natural Selection

If the continuous and discontinuous variation in a population has a genetic basis then natural selection can act on that variation, leading to the evolution of new species.

Stabilising Selection

The most common way in which natural selection can act is **stabilising selection**. This is where the genetic diversity for a trait decreases over time, leading to a particular trait value becoming common. Rather than extreme traits being favoured, intermediate variants are selected for.

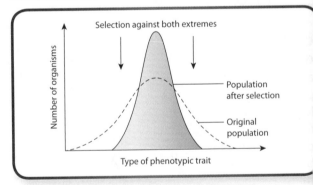

An example of stabilising selection is the birth weight of human babies. Babies that are born with too low a birth weight have a higher surface area to volume ratio and therefore lose heat more rapidly and also become ill more easily. Babies with a larger weight are more difficult to pass through the mother's pelvis. Stabilising selection has led to babies having a medium birth weight.

Directional Selection

In **directional selection**, there is positive selection for individuals possessing a particular trait. As time passes and the selective pressure remains the number of individuals with the particular trait increases until it becomes the norm for the population.

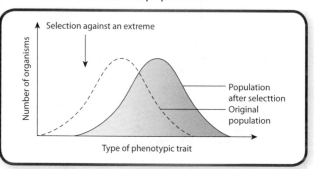

An example is selection for longer neck length in giraffes. As more giraffes eat the lower-hanging leaves on trees, those with genes for a longer neck are selected for, as they have access to more leaves. Over time, those with genes for a shorter neck decrease as the longer necked giraffes are in a better position to compete.

Disruptive Selection

When natural selection favours both extremes of variation, it is called disruptive selection. Over time the two extreme variants become more common whereas the intermediate states become less common or lost altogether.

Genetic Drift

Genetic drift is a basic, random process that leads to a change in the frequency that an allele appears in the population. It is not caused by natural selection but leads to a change in the number of alleles available for natural selection to act upon. In each generation of a population, just by chance some individuals leave behind more offspring with a given allele than others that carry an alternative allele. The next generation now has more individuals that have the given allele rather than the alternative. Purely by chance the number of individuals with the alternative decreases. If this happens often then eventually it is possible for the alternative allele to disappear from a population.

The effect of genetic drift is greater in small populations.

Genetic Bottleneck

Genetic bottleneck describes a sharp reduction in the size of a population due to a significant environmental change. If the majority of a population possesses similar alleles for a given trait, if there is a significant environmental change that affects carriers of that trait then the number of individuals in the population with that trait can be reduced significantly.

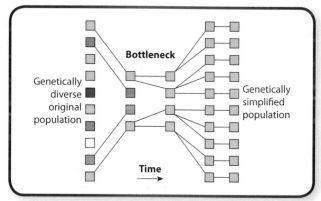

The environmental change causes a reduction in diversity as only a small part of the population that has the alleles to survive lives and passes on its genes to the next generation. The next generation has less variation than the original population.

An example of a genetic bottleneck in a living population is the cheetah, which was reduced to a small population size about 12 000 years ago during the last ice age. This led to the population becoming isolated in Africa and having a much reduced genetic diversity.

Founder Effect

The **founder effect** describes the loss of genetic variation that occurs when a new population is established from a very small number of individuals from a larger population. It is similar to a genetic bottleneck only in this case there is no environmental effect acting on the populations; the organisms instead leave the population.

The founders cannot carry all of the available alleles of the starting population. Therefore they bring a smaller selection of alleles.

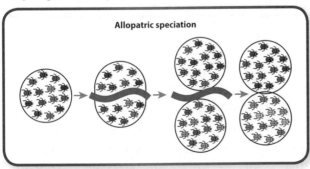

DAY 6

Isolating Mechanisms

Isolating mechanisms are the characteristics of a species that reduce or prevent successful sexual reproduction with members of other populations of that species. Over time this can lead to speciation.

Allopatric Speciation

Allopatric speciation occurs when members of a species become separated into geographically isolated populations that can no longer interbreed. Allopatric speciation can occur when a physical barrier occurs, e.g. a new river or the movement of land masses through plate tectonics. This means that the pool of alleles in each population is isolated. Genetic drift, the founder effect and natural selection can significantly alter the alleles present in both populations. If, when reunited, the members of the populations can no longer breed to produce fertile offspring, then they will have become new species.

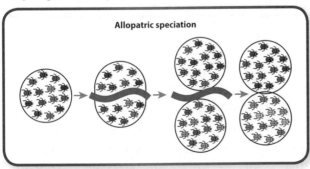

Allopatric speciation

Sympatric Speciation

Sympatric speciation occurs when new species evolve from a single ancestral species in the same geographic region. An example here is the apple maggot fly in the USA. Apple maggot flies used to lay eggs on hawthorn, a tree native to America. When the domestic apple was introduced some apple maggot fly females laid their eggs on the apples. Female apple maggot flies lay their eggs on the type of fruit they grew up in, so there were then separate populations growing up on the two different types of fruit. Over a long period of time significant differences occurred, leading to the formation of new species.

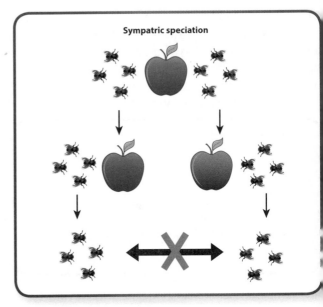

Sympatric speciation

Sympatric speciation also occurs when there are chromosomal abnormalities, e.g. an extra chromosome is copied or one is lost. If there is more than one individual with the same chromosomal abnormality, and they can interbreed, then a new species can form.

QUICK TEST

1. What type of variation is plotted using a histogram?

2. What type of variation is coded for by only one or two genes?

3. What is the most common type of natural selection?

4. Draw a graph to illustrate this form of selection.

5. Which is an example of directional selection: neck length of giraffes or birth weight of babies?

6. Explain how directional selection works.

7. Draw a graph to illustrate directional selection.

8. What is genetic drift?

9. What is the name given to a sharp reduction in the size of a population due to a significant environmental change?

10. What are allopatric and sympatric speciation?

- Continuous variation is where there is no limit on the value for a characteristic (or phenotypic trait) in a population. It is caused by the interaction of many genes, along with environmental factors. Examples include weight and height.

- Discontinuous variation is where a characteristic is coded for by one or two genes. It is not affected by the environment so the trait fits into distinct categories.

- Variation in a population allows natural selection to act to influence a phenotypic trait in the population, leading to the evolution of a new species.

- Stabilising selection is the most common form of selection. Genetic diversity for a trait decreases over time, leading to a particular trait becoming common. Intermediate variants are favoured.

- Directional selection is where there is positive selection for individuals possessing a particular trait. Over time it becomes the norm for the population.

- Genetic drift is a basic, random process leading to a change in allele frequency. It is not caused by natural selection but leads to the change of allele frequency that natural selection can act upon.

- Some individuals through chance breed more individuals with an allele than those with the alternative allele. Over time the alternative version may end up disappearing.

- A genetic bottleneck is a sharp reduction in population size due to a significant environmental change. This can lead to a big reduction in individuals with a trait.

- The founder effect describes the loss of genetic variation that occurs when a new population is established from a very small number of individuals.

- Allopatric speciation is where species get separated into geographic populations that cannot breed.

- Sympatric speciation is where new species evolve in the same geographic region, whereby a new behaviour may mean that members of the same species can no longer come together to mate.

PRACTICE QUESTIONS

In the USA the Northern elephant seal nearly became extinct in the late 1800s. The blubber is rich in oil and so the seals were actively hunted by whalers and sealers.

A small colony of between 20 and 100 survivors survived off the coast of Mexico's Baja California peninsula on Guadalupe Island. There are currently around 160 000 elephant seals on the island.

a) The elephant seals on Guadalupe island are an example of a genetic bottleneck.

    i) What is meant by the term genetic bottleneck? **[1 mark]**

    ii) What consequences will there be for the populations on Guadalupe island? **[2 marks]**

b) A group of elephant seals is discovered on another island 400 km away. Their traits are similar to those on Guadalupe Island but the range of variation is less. What effect is demonstrated by the seals that migrated to the new island? **[1 mark]**

c) The elephant seals on Guadalupe Island and the new island may eventually become new species. What type of speciation would this be an example of? **[1 mark]**

Analysing Experimental Results

When carrying out experiments it is important to realise that there is always random, chance variation. Before a conclusion can be made the data have to be analysed and checked to see whether the result is likely to be real or due to random chance. There are a wide variety of statistical tests that can help to make this assessment.

Standard Deviation

A very simple method of judging the validity of experimental data is to use the **standard deviation**. It measures the spread of data around the mean. It is particularly useful for comparing sets of data that have the same mean but for which the range of values making up the mean is different. A larger standard deviation indicates that the data are more varied for a given experiment.

Standard deviation (often denoted by the letter s) is calculated using the formula:

$$s = \sqrt{\frac{\sum(X - \bar{X})^2}{n - 1}}$$

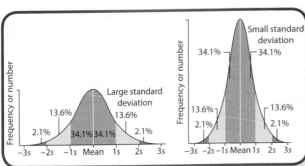

Where s = standard deviation, Σ = sum of, $\bar{X}$ = sample mean, X = sample value and n = number of samples making up the mean.

With experimental data it is expected that the data will form a bell-shaped curve around the mean.

Here each shaded area represents data that is one standard deviation away from the mean. If the data fit a normal distribution curve, then 68.2% of the sample should be within 1 standard deviation of the mean, 95.4% within 2 standard deviations of the mean and 99.6% within 3 standard deviations of the mean.

Chi-squared (χ^2) Test

The **chi-squared (χ^2) test** is one statistical method that can be used to determine whether a sample set of results

is likely to be representative of the true population. The test determines the probability that the difference between what has been observed in an experiment and what was expected in an experiment has occurred through chance alone. If the probability is high then the conclusion is that the obtained result occurred due to random chance alone. If the probability is low then the conclusion is that the difference observed is too high for chance alone and the effect observed is real. The test can be used when there are categorical data, e.g. phenotypes of offspring in a genetic cross.

Carrying Out the Test

The chi-squared (χ^2) test does not take the **mean** or **standard deviation** into account. It can be summarised as:

$$\chi^2 = \Sigma \frac{(Obs - Exp)^2}{Exp}$$

Where Obs is the observed result, e.g. the offspring counted with a particular phenotype, and Exp is the expected result, e.g. the offspring you expect to have that phenotype.

To carry out a chi-squared test the following steps are followed.

1. State the **null hypothesis**. In this experiment, the null hypothesis is that there is no difference between the observed and expected offspring.

2. Calculate the probability of each expected phenotype.

3. Calculate the expected number of each phenotype.

4. Calculate the value of χ^2.

5. Work out the degrees of freedom: here, this is the number of phenotype groups minus 1.

6. Compare the calculated value of χ^2 with the table value, for the given degrees of freedom.

If the differences between the observed and expected values are low, then χ^2 will be low.

If the differences between the observed and expected values are high, then χ^2 will be large.

The hypothesis is accepted if the χ^2 value is *less* than the table value and rejected if it is *greater* than the table value.

Worked Example

A plant breeder crosses a red flower with a white flower and obtains 100% red flowers. She then allows the red flowers to self-fertilise.

They produce 105 red flowers and 45 white flowers.

The assumption is that red must be dominant to white flowers. Using R to represent dominant red and r for recessive white, a Punnett square can be created of the first cross:

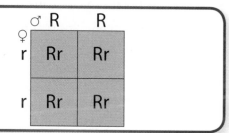

All of the offspring (the F_1 generation) are red. These flowers, which the plant breeder then self-pollinates, should in theory be all heterozygous red:

	♂ R	r
♀ R	RR	Rr
r	Rr	rr

The ratio of the offspring's phenotypes (the F_2 generation) should be 3:1 red to white.

Null hypothesis: there will be no difference between the observed and expected offspring.

There is a 75% chance of red and 25% chance of white in the offspring.

Phenotype	Observed	Expected
Red	105	$0.75 \times 150 = 112.5$
White	45	$0.25 \times 150 = 37.5$
Total	150	

$$\chi^2 = \Sigma \frac{(Obs - Exp)^2}{Exp}$$

$$\chi^2 = \frac{(105 - 112.5)^2}{112.5} + \frac{(45 - 37.5)^2}{37.5}$$

$$\chi^2 = \frac{56.25}{112.5} + \frac{56.25}{37.5}$$

$$\chi^2 = 0.5 + 1.5$$

$$\chi^2 = 2.0$$

5. Degrees of freedom = 1.

6. On a χ^2 table the value given at the 0.05 probability level is 3.841. The calculated χ^2 value is 2.0, which is less than 3.841. This means that the null hypothesis is accepted; the conclusion is that the differences between the observed and expected results are due to random variation and are not significant (at a 5% probability level).

Even though the result in this worked example has been accepted at the 5% probability level, it is important to bear in mind that this still means there is a 1 in 20 chance that the result is a false result.

Hardy–Weinberg Principle

The **Hardy–Weinberg principle** states that the allele and genotype frequencies in a population will remain constant from generation to generation, if other evolutionary pressures are absent. The principle is disrupted by mutations, natural selection, genetic drift and non-random mating. These factors are almost always present in a population, so the principle is in reality describing an ideal state.

The Hardy–Weinberg Equation

The Hardy–Weinberg principle is represented by an equation:

$$p^2 + 2pq + q^2 = 1$$

If, for a given gene, there are only two possible alleles, F and f, then in the Hardy–Weinberg equation p is the frequency of the F allele and q is the frequency of the f allele. This means that p^2 represents the frequency of the FF genotype, q^2 represents ff and $2pq$ represents $2 \times$ Ff.

In addition, the principle also means that $p + q = 1$.

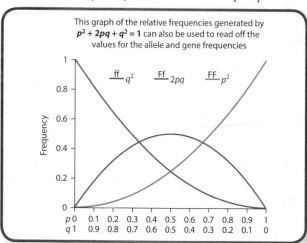

This graph of the relative frequencies generated by $p^2 + 2pq + q^2 = 1$ can also be used to read off the values for the allele and gene frequencies

The Hardy–Weinberg equation can be used to determine expected frequencies of allelic combinations, assuming no evolutionary pressures.

Worked Example

For example, a population has been sampled and the frequency of a homozygous recessive genotype (gg) is found to be 36%. What are the frequencies of the G and g alleles and the GG and Gg genotypes?

$$p^2 + 2pq + q^2 = 1$$

The frequency of gg is 36% (from the question). To calculate the frequency of the g allele, we use q^2.

$$q^2 = 0.36$$
$$q = \sqrt{0.36}$$
$$q = 0.6$$

This means the frequency of the g allele is 60% in the population.

As $q = 0.6$, using $p + q = 1$ then p must be 0.4, or 40% of the population.

The genotype GG is represented by p^2, so:

$$p^2 = 0.4^2$$
$$p^2 = 0.16$$

So, 16% of the population have the GG genotype.

The heterozygous phenotype is given by $2pq$, so:

$$2pq = 2(0.4 \times 0.6)$$
$$2pq = 0.48$$

Which means that 48% of the population is heterozygous, Gg.

SUMMARY

- **Experimental results always contain random, chance variation. Before data can be used to support a conclusion they have to be analysed to see whether the result is real or due to random chance.**

- **A wide variety of tests can be carried out to help make this assessment.**

- **Standard deviation is a way to judge variability around the mean. The larger the deviation, the greater the samples vary from the mean.**

- **The chi-squared (χ^2) test determines whether a sample set of results is likely to be representative of the true population. It determines the probability that the difference between what has been observed and what was expected in an experiment has occurred through chance alone. It does not take the mean into account.**

- **The chi-squared (χ^2) test can be summarised as:**

$$\chi^2 = \Sigma \frac{(\text{Obs} - \text{Exp})^2}{\text{Exp}}$$

- **Obs is the offspring counted with a particular phenotype; Exp is the expected offspring that would have that phenotype.**

- **To carry out a chi-squared test:**
  - **state the null hypothesis**
  - **calculate the probability of each expected phenotype and the expected number of each phenotype**
  - **calculate the value of χ^2, work out the degrees of freedom (the number of groups minus 1)**
  - **compare the calculated value of χ^2 with the table value, for the given degrees of freedom.**

- **The Hardy–Weinberg principle states that the allele and genotype frequencies in a population will remain constant from generation to generation, if other evolutionary pressures are absent.**

- **The principle is represented by the equation:**

$$p^2 + 2pq + q^2 = 1$$

- The Hardy–Weinberg principle is disrupted by: mutations, natural selection, genetic drift, non-random mating.
- These factors are almost always present in a population, so the principle is in reality describing an ideal state.

QUICK TEST

1. What does the chi-squared (χ^2) test determine?

2. What do the terms Obs and Exp refer to in the chi-squared (χ^2) test?

3. What is the null hypothesis in the chi-squared (χ^2) test?

4. How is the degrees of freedom calculated?

5. What is the Hardy–Weinberg principle?

6. What is the Hardy–Weinberg equation?

7. If the frequency of a dominant genotype DD is 24%, what is the frequency of the D and d alleles?

8. What will be the frequency in the population of the homozygous recessive dd?

9. What would the frequency of heterozygous individuals be?

10. What factors can affect the Hardy–Weinberg principle?

PRACTICE QUESTIONS

. Banded snails of the species *Cepaea nemoralis* have coloured shells. The gene for shell colour S has three alleles.

Colour of shell	Allele	Dominance
Brown	S^B	Dominant to S^P and S^Y
Pink	S^P	Dominant to S^Y
Yellow	S^Y	Recessive

a) The alleles for brown and pink are **not** codominant. Explain what would be seen if they were.　[2 marks]

b) Write all the genotypes that would result in a snail with a brown shell.　[1 mark]

c) *Cepaea nemoralis* can have bands. The banding is controlled by a single gene with two alleles. The allele for unbanded shells (B) is dominant to the allele for banded shells (b).

A population of snails contained 56% unbanded snails. What percentage of the population would be expected to be heterozygous for banding? Show your working.　[4 marks]

DNA Sequencing

DNA sequencing is the process by which the precise order of nucleotides in a DNA molecule can be determined. This enables the sequence of a gene, chromosome or genome to be mapped. The results from DNA sequencing can be used in molecular biology to identify genes and the proteins that they encode. This technique is used in evolutionary biology to map changes in organisms and to create phylogenetic trees. In medicine the results can be used to identify causes of disease and ways for the diseases to be treated. Forensic science utilises DNA sequences to provide evidence for guilt or innocence.

Principles of DNA Sequencing

DNA sequencing can be carried out using enzymes or by chemical degradation. The enzyme-based method, called Sanger sequencing, after Frederick Sanger who invented it in the 1970s, was widely used but has now been replaced by next-generation technologies. The Sanger chain-termination method uses enzymes called **restriction enzymes** (or **restriction endonucleases**) to cut the DNA into fragments ending at the four bases: adenine (A), guanine (G), cytosine (C) and thymine (T). It uses a single-stranded DNA sample with the sequence to be determined (a DNA **primer**), an enzyme to synthesise a complementary strand to the sample (DNA polymerase), normal **deoxynucleoside triphosphates** (dNTPs) and modified **dideoxynucleoside triphosphates** (ddNTPs). The ddNTPs terminate DNA strand elongation. The base component of each ddNTP is shown below. The modified ddNTPs are different because they are unable to form chemical links to any other dNTPs.

ddNTP name	Corresponding base
ddTTP	T
ddATP	A
ddGTP	G
ddCTP	C

The DNA sample is divided into four reactions, each containing all four normal dNTPs but only one of the four strand-terminating ddNTPs.

In each of the four reactions, successive rounds of heating and cooling allow DNA polymerase to make a large number of extensions of the primer that have a sequence complementary to the DNA sample. Fragments of different sizes are formed because the elongation is only stopped by random inclusion of a ddNTP. The different sized fragments are removed from the sample strand by heat, and separated by size.

In the past, detection of the fragments was achieved using radioactivity. Nowadays, this method has been replaced by fluorescence detection, which takes advantage of the fact of fluorescence emitted from each different ddNTP. This is far safer but the main advantage is that there is no need to keep the reactants separated in four tubes, because the fluorescent signal for each ddNTP is unique. This has made the process quicker and allowed it to become fully automated, enabling the entire human genome to be sequenced by 2003.

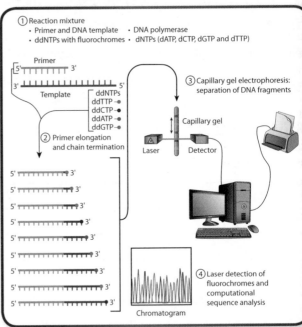

There are now a variety of methods of analysing DNA sequences, called **next-generation sequencing**. These speed the process of amplification further, enabling a human genome to be sequenced in as little as 26 hours.

Uses of DNA Sequencing

The development of rapid, cost-effective and safe methods of DNA sequencing has led to the new fields of bioinformatics and computational biology. These fields enable the creation of **phylogenetic trees** so hat the relationship of one species to another can be mapped. If extinct organisms have DNA that can be analysed, the evolutionary relationships of extinct to extant (i.e. still living) species can be investigated. It is also possible to examine genotype–phenotype relationships, seeing how the genotype is expressed as phenotype in living organisms.

Rapid testing can also help in **epidemiology**, both in rapidly identifying the cause of a disease and in tracking how and where it has come from.

DNA Profiling

One of the most significant applications of DNA sequencing is **DNA profiling**. This involves taking certain regions of DNA that are very likely to be different in unrelated individuals. These sequences are called variable-number tandem repeats (or VNTRs) and are unlikely to be the same in any two people other than a pair of identical twins. This means that DNA can be isolated, amplified and profiled from a crime scene (when it is often called DNA fingerprinting). If a suspect's DNA matches, then it is very unlikely that it belongs to another person. Of course, there could be other reasons for the presence of the DNA and the test itself gives a probability that there is a match.

In the figure, DNA from a crime scene is compared with that of three suspects. The VNTRs are identified from DNA samples using radiolabelled probes and the DNA is cut up using endonucleases. DNA fragments containing the VNTRs are separated by electrophoresis. The `fingerprint' that matches the one at the crime scene belongs to the culprit (Suspect 2).

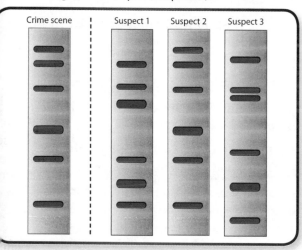

There are a number of high-profile cases where DNA analysis of the historical evidence from the crime scene has proved that the person convicted could not have committed the crime.

DNA profiling is also used to help establish parentage by comparing the DNA sequence of a child with that of the parents to determine if they really are the parents.

DNA profiling is now being used in other industries, such as the food industry. In 2013 the Food Standards Agency checked the DNA of many food products purporting to be made from beef and discovered that many were actually made from horse meat.

Synthetic Biology

DNA sequencing and the understanding of the function of the genome has led to the development of synthetic organisms. These are cells that have a genome that has been built by humans assembling the sequences of certain key genes and inserting them into a cell that is devoid of its own genetic material. The first such cell was reported in 2010. In 2015 the first self-replicating synthetic **protocell** was reported. This is not a living cell, but a sphere that contains DNA and the machinery needed for replication. Under certain changes in pH the protocells are able to divide once. The protocells cannot continue to divide as a normal cell would because they cannot restock the cellular machinery, which normal cells do in the S phase of the cell cycle.

Polymerase Chain Reaction (PCR)

The amount of DNA at a crime scene is often very small, so an effective way to increase the amount of DNA is needed. The polymerase chain reaction (or PCR) amplifies (makes more copies of) DNA. DNA is first denatured to separate it into two strands. Primers are then added during the annealing phase. A type of DNA polymerase that isn't denatured by heat (called *Taq* polymerase) lengthens the new DNA chains through the addition of nucleotides, leading to the formation of new strands of DNA. The process is repeated until there are millions of copies of the DNA. The different stages of the method have different temperature requirements and can now be fully automated.

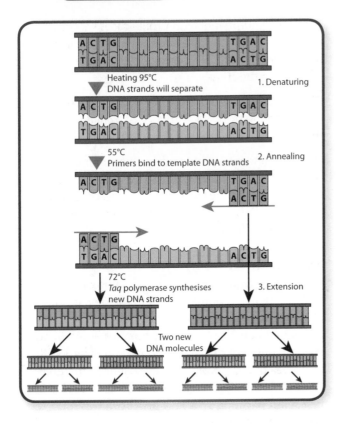

1. Denaturing

Heating 95°C
DNA strands will separate

2. Annealing

55°C
Primers bind to template DNA strands

72°C
Taq polymerase synthesises
new DNA strands

3. Extension

Two new
DNA molecules

QUICK TEST

1. Through what process can the precise order of nucleotides in DNA be determined?

2. What does dNTP stand for?

3. Give the names of the four DNA dNTPs.

4. What property of ddNTPs makes them so useful in sequencing?

5. Complete the following: Attaching fluorescent markers to ddNTPs is an advantage because ….

6. Describe the process of DNA fingerprinting.

7. How is sequencing used in bioinformatics and computational biology?

8. What is synthetic biology?

9. What is PCR?

10. How is DNA profiling used in the food industry?

SUMMARY

- The precise order of nucleotides in DNA can be determined by DNA sequencing. From this the sequence of a gene, chromosome or genome can be mapped.

- DNA sequencing takes advantage of the fact that DNA uses complementary base pairing. Fragments of the entire DNA sequence will always contain the same bases. If every possible fragment is collected then the entire sequence of DNA can be worked out.

- Fluorescence DNA sequencing involves taking a primer (a starting section of DNA with a short, 20-base sequence) and adding DNA polymerase, nucleotides with normal bases (dNTPs) and specific replication-stopping nucleotides (ddNTPs).

- Each ddNTP has a different fluorescent signature that enables it to be recognised by computer.

- The strand of DNA will form normally until one of the four ddNTPs is attached. This is a random process, so thousands of different-length molecules will be created.

- The earliest methods of DNA sequencing involved radiolabelling the ddNTP. This meant the experiment had to be done four times as the four ddNTPs could not be mixed together.

- The process is now automated with the fragments produced passing through a fluorescence detector. The samples are then analysed by computer to work out the original sequence. Using fluorescence means that the entire experiment can be carried out once in the same vessel, making it faster and more accurate.

- Bioinformatics and computational biology make use of DNA sequencing to identify the relationships between extinct and living organisms, compiling phylogenetic trees. Rapid testing can now be used in epidemiology to determine the cause of a disease and its origin. Medical treatments can be formulated based on an understanding of a disease organism.

- DNA profiling involves sequencing DNA from regions that are very likely to be different in non-related individuals. These variable-number tandem repeats (VNTRs) can be isolated, amplified and profiled, giving a 'DNA barcode'.

- With DNA profiling, DNA from crime scenes can be compared with DNA from suspects, to either prove guilt or exonerate. Paternity testing uses the same principles to establish who the real parents of a child are.

- Synthetic biology involves assembling genes and inserting them into a 'dead' cell.

- The polymerase chain reaction (PCR) is used to amplify very small amounts of DNA by replication. The DNA sample is denatured into single strands and then new strands formed. The process is repeated until the required amount of DNA has been made.

PRACTICE QUESTIONS

1. The first DNA sequencing methods involved using radioactively labelled ddNTPs (the Sanger method).

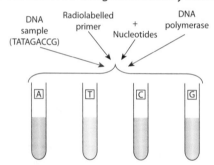

Four test tubes were labelled with A, T, C and G. Into each tube were placed: the DNA sample to be sequenced, the four dNTP nucleotides and the enzyme DNA polymerase.

Into each tube a specific ddNTP was added at about 1% the concentration of the normal dNTP nucelotides. The tubes were left to allow the DNA polymerase to work. This led to a range of different DNA molecules ranging from the full-length sequence to very short fragments. In tube A all fragments stop at an A ddNTP, in tube T all the fragments stop at a T ddNTP.

The contents of the tubes were then run side by side on an electrophoresis gel.

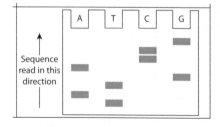

a) What is the DNA sequence indicated by this technique? [1 mark]

b) What is the modern way of identifying the ddNTP nucleotides and how is this an advantage over the earlier technique? [3 marks]

Genetic Engineering

Genetic engineering involves the isolation of a gene coding for a desired trait and the insertion of the gene into a new organism that does not currently possess that trait. There are a variety of methods for getting the gene into the target organism. Most involve the use of a **vector**, a plasmid or an organism such as a virus that can pass on the DNA sequence.

Recombinant DNA

'Recombinant' DNA molecules are those that have been created in the laboratory. They can be used to move genetic material from different sources into an organism, enabling proteins to be formed that are not normally found in that organism's genome. Recombinant DNA can be produced using several methods.

- Restriction enzymes (restriction endonucleases) are used to cut the desired gene from the DNA of a donor organism and transfer it to the target organism.
- mRNA can be converted to complementary DNA (cDNA) using **reverse transcriptase**, an enzyme originally discovered in retroviruses.
- In 2015 a new technology, a 'gene machine', was introduced. This machine automates the process of piecing the nucleotides of the recombinant DNA together in the desired order.

Restriction Endonucleases

Having identified the gene from the donor organism, various restriction endonucleases are used that specifically target nucleotide sequences. Each restriction endonuclease targets a different base sequence. The restriction endonucleases cut the DNA at that point, producing DNA fragments.

The enzyme *Eco*RI cuts the sequence GAATTC, producing fragments with 'sticky' ends (ends made of single-stranded DNA):

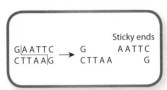

In contrast, *Sma*I cuts the sequence CCCGGG, producing 'blunt' ends (ends of double-stranded DNA):

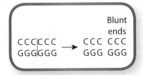

DNA Amplification and Insertion

Whichever method has been used to create the recombinant DNA, once the correct DNA sequence has been extracted or created, the DNA has to be amplified. This is achieved through PCR, which is an *in vitro* method. Alternatively, the new DNA sequence can be inserted into vectors (such as bacteria and viruses) which will then replicate the molecules *in vivo*. Promoter and terminator regions must first be added to the DNA fragments. The restriction endonucleases have to cut the DNA of the vector so that the introduced DNA will slot in. **DNA ligase** is then used to join the DNA together.

The vector is then introduced into the host. If successful, the host cell will be transformed and will contain the recombinant DNA. It is important to add additional marker genes so that host cells that have been successfully transformed can be identified. There are two types of marker gene. A selectable marker gives the host the protection from a treatment that would normally kill it, e.g. antibiotic resistance. The second type of marker is called a screenable marker. These make the host cells possessing the gene appear different, e.g. fluorescing under UV light.

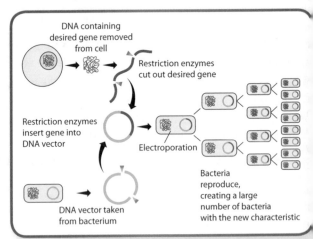

An example would be taking the gene that codes for the production of human insulin and inserting it into the DNA of a plasmid (the vector). The plasmid is then placed into the bacterium through **electroporation**. Electroporation involves applying an electric field across a cell. This makes it more permeable to larger molecules. The plasmid can then be introduced to the

...cterial cell. There it will reproduce until all bacteria ...ossess the plasmid and therefore have the ability to ...oduce human insulin.

...ene Therapy

...ere is the potential to use genetic engineering ...chniques to help cure genetic disorders. If a person ...s a defective gene that causes a genetic condition ...s theoretically possible to introduce a working ...py of the gene into the person's cells. The working ...ne would then produce the correct or missing ...olypeptide. This is called somatic cell gene therapy. ...is currently legal as the genes that are affected are ...t passed on to the person's offspring.

...ternatively, the deficient gene could in theory be ...moved and replaced in the cells that produce the ...ametes or the gametes themselves. The gametes ...ould therefore carry the functioning gene. This ...ould be a way of removing certain alleles that cause ...evastating genetic conditions. This is currently not ...gal in the UK as the introduced genes will be passed ...n to future generations.

...thics

...ere are arguments for and against using genetic ...chnologies to modify organisms. The production ...f human insulin is an example of '**pharming**'. ...his is where pharmaceuticals are produced by ...ganisms that have been genetically engineered. ...ior to this insulin had to be taken from pigs. This ...aused problems for vegans with diabetes and ...ose whose religion banned pork. Ethically there ...s a dilemma: should animals be altered to produce ...harmaceuticals? On the one hand it can save many ...ves, including those of animals that need similar ...eatments. On the other hand the organism that is ...eing pharmed may suffer.

...isease resistance can help a plant or animal survive. ...his leads to a greater crop or a larger quantity of ...od product, However, there is a risk that the gene ...r the resistance could enter the wild population. ...his could cause a disturbance to the food chains ...nd the food web. For example, genetically modified ...GM) soya was introduced in 1994. The arguments for ...e genetic modification were that the oil produced ...ould be of a better quality. The modification reduced ...e amount of linolenic acid, a compound that ...mpairs the quality of the oil. Arguments against were

that the gene could enter other plants and affect food chains. Another argument was that the company making the GM soya would profit too much whereas the farmers who could not afford the GM soya would lose business.

Cloning

Clones are organisms that are genetically identical. They occur naturally; for example, identical twins are clones formed from the splitting of the embryo in the first few cell divisions. Strawberry plants produce clones through runners. In horticulture it is common to produce clones of plants. The clones will have identical properties and the grower can ensure consistency in the final product. Cloning in plants is achieved through various propagation techniques.

Cuttings

Many plants can be propagated by taking a cutting. The addition of a plant growth regulator stimulates the growth of roots.

Plant Tissue Culture

It is possible to create large numbers of plant clones using very small amounts of tissue. Growing the tissue samples in a growth medium containing growth regulators leads to the production of seedlings that can then be planted.

One issue with cultivating a crop where the plants are genetically identical is that the plants are more susceptible to disease. One disease can affect all individuals as they are all equally susceptible.

Animal Clones

Artificial cloning can occur either by artificial embryo twinning or through enucleation and then **somatic cell nuclear transfer (SCNT)**.

Embryo Twinning

Twins can be artificially created by deliberately dividing an embryo into two and then implanting the embryos into surrogate mothers.

Enucleation and Somatic Cell Nuclear Transfer

Enucleation is the removal of the nucleus from an egg cell. This leaves a cell that has the machinery for cell division but not the genetic material.

The next step is to take the nucleus of one of the somatic cells and transfer it to the cell that is nucleus free. The donor nucleus is inserted into the egg and then an electric current applied that stimulates cell division. This process is repeated a number of times as it does not have a high success rate.

The figure shows the creation of Dolly the sheep. Dolly, originally named 6LL3, was the first mammal cloned from an adult body cell, a cell from the udder.

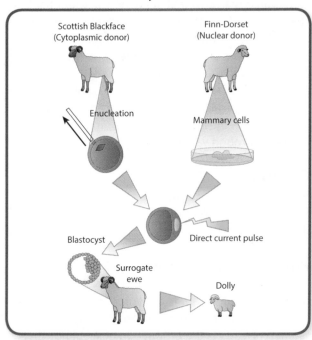

When cell division takes place and an embryo forms it is then implanted into the uterus of a surrogate mother. The mother will often have very obvious differences to the donor animal. This helps to check whether the animal that is born is the clone of the donor rather than a hidden pregnancy of the surrogate.

Cloning Efficacy

The efficacy of cloning is still being investigated. The success rate of births from SCNT methods is very low, so it is not an efficient way of producing animals.

It may be better to carry out selective breeding instead. In addition, although the genomes of the clones are the same as the animals they were cloned from, there is evidence that clones age faster than non-clones. This means that the lifespan of the clone animals is shorter than that of non-clones.

Animal cloning can be used to replicate animals that have desired traits. Examples include a cow that produces low-cholesterol milk or a race horse that has won a lot of races. The question is, are the clones that are produced worth the cost as well as the lives of the unsuccessful offspring created?

QUICK TEST

1. What type of enzyme is used to remove a target gene from an organism?

2. Describe how this type of enzyme works.

3. What types of vectors are suitable for genetic engineering?

4. How is the target gene inserted into the vector?

5. What is electroporation?

6. What advantages are there in creating bacteria that can express human insulin?

7. Why is somatic gene therapy legal in the UK?

8. What is cloning?

9. What are the two methods of creating clones of animals?

10. What are the risks of cloning crop plants?

SUMMARY

- Genetic engineering is where a gene for a desired trait is inserted into an organism that lacks the trait.

- To create recombinant DNA, the gene must first be identified and then removed from the host organism. This involves using restriction enzymes (restriction endonucleases) that cut DNA when they encounter a specific nucleotide sequence. There are many types of restriction enzyme, each targeting different sequences of nucleotides.

- The DNA of a vector (e.g. a bacterial plasmid) is cut using the same restriction enzymes. The desired gene is then inserted into the vector DNA using the enzyme DNA ligase.

- Electroporation is used to make the bacterial cell surface membrane more permeable to large proteins. The plasmids are then introduced to the bacterial cell.

- The plasmids and bacteria reproduce until all have the desired gene and express it.

- The gene for making human insulin is inserted into bacteria in this way. The bacteria can then produce human insulin that can be collected, purified and given to people with diabetes.

- Gene therapy is the potential for genetic engineering to help cure genetic disorders. If a person has a defective gene that causes a genetic condition, then a working copy of the gene could be inserted. The working gene would then produce the correct or missing polypeptide. This is called somatic gene therapy and is legal in the UK as the genes involved are not passed on to offspring.

- A faulty gene could also be theoretically removed and replaced in the cells producing gametes. This is not currently legal in the UK as the introduced genes would be passed on to future generations.

- There are arguments for and against using genetic technology to modify organisms.

- Human insulin production is an example of 'pharming'.

- Prior to genetic engineering insulin had to be extracted from pigs, which posed an ethical dilemma.

- Adding genes for disease resistance could help a plant or animal survive, increasing yield. But if the gene were to escape into the environment into natural populations then food chains and webs could be disrupted.

- Cloning involves making identical copies of organisms that all have the same desired traits. In plants, clones can be made using cuttings and adding root hormone powder to encourage root growth. Tissue culture can be used to generate a large number of clones using small tissue samples.

- With animals, clones can be made by artificially forming twins or through enucleation followed by somatic cell nuclear transfer (SCNT). The success rate from SCNT is not very high and the clones have a shorter lifespan than non-clones.

PRACTICE QUESTIONS

1. The shortage of vitamin A is estimated to kill around 680 000 children under the age of 5 each year. Golden Rice™ is a genetically engineered rice that has three genes coding for beta-carotene, a precursor to vitamin A, inserted into the chromosome. The edible parts of the rice then produce beta-carotene.

   As of 2016 Golden Rice has not been grown commercially anywhere in the world.

   a) Discuss the potential *benefits* of growing Golden Rice.   [2 marks]

   b) Golden Rice was first produced in 2000. Suggest why, as of 2016, Golden Rice has not been grown commercially anywhere in the world.   [3 marks]

   c) The Golden Rice is produced using recombinant DNA.

   i) What is recombinant DNA?   [1 mark]

   ii) What enzyme is used to remove the one of the genes coding for beta-carotene from daffodils?   [1 mark]

   iii) What enzyme is then used to insert the beta-carotene gene into the rice DNA?   [1 mark]

Biotechnology

Microorganisms are used in **biotechnological processes**, which include brewing, baking, cheese-making, yoghurt production, insulin production and bioremediation (which uses microorganisms to break down wastes and pollutants). Microorganisms are used because they grow rapidly and can be contained easily. They can be purified so that the end product is always the same. Under ideal conditions they grow quickly and have a short life cycle. The genomes of many important microorganisms are sequenced, so there are no surprises as to what the organism can produce. They can be genetically modified to produce desired polypeptides easily, without the ethical considerations that would come with using an animal such as a cow. Economically it is easier to grow and maintain cultures of microorganisms than to grow other animals. They are simpler than larger animals so they do not have such demanding living requirements, and thus costs can be kept down.

Microorganisms for Food Production

Microorganisms have been involved in food production for thousands of years. Alcohol is produced by anaerobic fermentation in yeast. Cheese is made by the action of bacteria such as *Lactobacillus* spp. *Streptococcus* spp. are used to convert lactose in milk to lactic acid, lowering the milk's pH.

The advantages of using microorganisms for food production include:

- production of protein far faster than plants or animals can produce it
- production can be easily altered according to demand
- vegetarians can eat the protein (there is no animal matter).

Disadvantages include:

- people may not want to eat fungal or bacterial products that are grown on waste
- protein has to be purified to ensure there are no contaminants
- the conditions for the growth of microorganisms are also ideal for pathogenic microorganisms
- the texture of proteins produced in this way is different to that of animal and plant protein.

Culturing Microorganisms

To ensure that only a desired microorganism is cultured and not a **pathogenic**, unwanted microorganism, **aseptic techniques** have to be used. This involves sterilisation of all equipment before use, including the nutrient growth medium into which the microorganism will be introduced. The growth medium will be either created as a batch process or provided continuously via continuous culture.

Batch Culture

Batch culture involves introducing the microorganism into a closed-loop system. Microbial growth is divided into four stages. The **lag phase** is where the microorganisms have not yet affected the chemical environment that they have been introduced into. The **logarithmic growth phase** (often called the log phase) occurs when the introduced microorganisms grow rapidly. The microorganisms initially have ideal growth conditions so growth is **exponential**. The population reaches a point where the population growth is matched by the death of microorganisms. This is the **stationary phase**. Once the ideal conditions have deteriorated, e.g. there is lack of a nutrient or a build up of a waste product, then the growth enters a period of decline, the death or **logarithmic decline phase**.

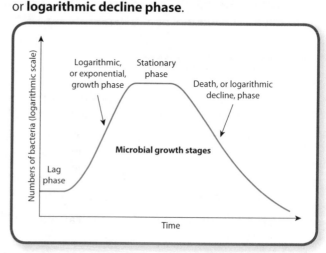

The waste produced may or may not be useful. For example, in brewing the waste product of fermentation is alcohol, which is a desired product.

Growing microorganisms in batch culture is relatively simple. Once the product has been harvested then the system has to be cleaned thoroughly and resterilised before being set up again.

Continuous Culture

The advantage of continuous culture systems is that they can produce a product for as long as the growth conditions can be maintained. Continuous culture involves an open system where the product can be removed and new growth media introduced. This means that the death or logarithmic phase is never reached because the ideal conditions are kept constant. Continuous culture systems are more complicated than batch culturing. The system has to be continuously monitored and the conditions adjusted via negative feedback. If the temperature increases, the culture vessel is cooled; if the number of microorganisms increases above a set level then some are removed, and so on.

The vessels used for continuous culture are called **bioreactors** or biofermenters.

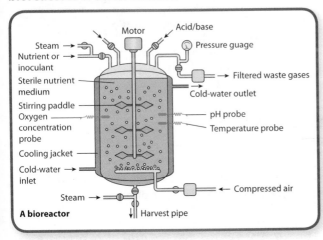

A bioreactor

Immobilised Enzymes

Enzymes can be immobilised on an inert, insoluble material. The benefit of immobilising enzymes is that they gain improved resistance to changes in pH and temperature. The enzymes are also easily separated from the reaction products and reused after the reaction, which means they can be used again more rapidly.

There are a variety of different ways to immobilise enzymes.

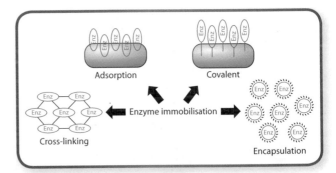

Adsorption is where the enzyme is attached to the outside of the inert material. Adsorption is not a chemical process, so the attachment is not regular. This method can lead to the active site of the enzyme being blocked on a proportion of the adsorbed molecules, so it is not as efficient as other methods.

Covalent immobilisation is where the enzyme is bound covalently to an inert support material. This is the strongest type of immobilisation as the enzyme is very unlikely to leave the support.

In cross-linking the enzymes are all covalently linked to one another, providing a matrix made up of enzyme. The active site is always available, making this an effective method.

Encapsulation involves the enzyme being effectively trapped inside insoluble beads. The insoluble substance can hinder the entry of the reactants and exit of the substrate.

Enzymes can be immobilised on an inert, insoluble material such as calcium alginate. Calcium alginate balls are made by reacting sodium alginate with calcium carbonate.

Cats should not drink cows' milk because they are lactose intolerant. A simple way to produce milk suitable for cats is to convert the lactose into the monosaccharides glucose and galactose.

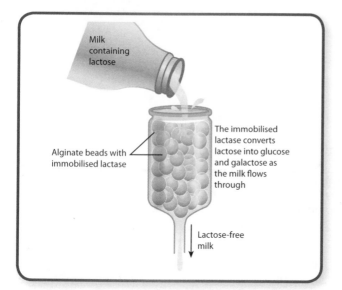

Milk containing lactose

Alginate beads with immobilised lactase

The immobilised lactase converts lactose into glucose and galactose as the milk flows through

Lactose-free milk

When the alginate beads are being created, the enzyme lactase is added so that each bead contains the enzyme. As the milk trickles through the beads, lactase breaks down the lactose. The milk that is produced can then be tested, using lactose detection strips. The lactase remains within the bead, so does not leave in the milk.

QUICK TEST

1. Why is the way in which microorganisms grow a reason for their biotechnological use?

2. What is the ethical advantage of using microorganisms in biotechnology?

3. Give two advantages of using microorganisms to produce food.

4. Give two disadvantages of using microorganisms to produce food.

5. Why are aseptic techniques used?

6. Draw and label the typical growth curve for a bacterial batch culture.

7. What is continuous culture?

8. What advantages do continuous culture methods have over batch methods?

9. What is enzyme immobilisation?

10. What advantages are there with enzyme immobilisation?

SUMMARY

● Biotechnological processes make use of microorganisms because microbes grow rapidly with a short life cycle and are easily contained. They can be purified so the end product is always the same.

● Microbial genomes can be sequenced so there are no surprises as to what the organism produces. They can be genetically modified to produce a desired polypeptide without ethical barriers.

● Economically it is cheaper to grow and maintain cultures of microorganisms compared to larger organisms.

● Microorganisms have been used in food production for thousands of years. For example, alcohol is produced through anaerobic fermentation in yeast and cheese is made by bacteria such as *Lactobaccillus* spp. and *Streptococcus* spp.

● Advantages include:
   • faster protein production compared to plants and animals
   • production suits demand
   • vegetarians can eat the protein produced.

- **Disadvantages include:**
  - lack of public appetite for products grown on waste
  - protein has to be purified
  - conditions being ideal for pathogens
  - different texture of the protein compared to animal and plant protein.
- Aseptic techniques have to be used when culturing microorganisms to prevent contamination.
- Batch culture is where the microorganism is grown in a closed-loop system.
- The microorganisms go through a set pattern of growth phases: lag, logarithmic (log) or exponential growth, stationary and death or decline phase.
- Once the product has been harvested, the equipment is washed, sterilised and the process restarted.
- Continuous culture involves using bioreactors that supply continual nutrients and remove products before the death or decline phase is reached. More effort is required to monitor all aspects of the incubation process (temperature, pH, O_2 levels, etc.).
- Instead of microorganisms, enzymes can be immobilised on an inert, insoluble material.
- The enzymes have improved resistance to pH and temperature changes and are easy to remove from the reaction once it has finished.
- Enzymes can be attached to an inert material (adsorption), covalently bonded, cross-linked in a matrix or encapsulated (trapped inside the support material, e.g. a bead).

PRACTICE QUESTIONS

1. There are a number of ways to immobilise enzymes for biotechnological use. One is to add the enzyme to calcium alginate beads. The calcium alginate is inert and insoluble. Lactose-free milk can be produced using the enzyme lactase immobilised onto calcium alginate beads. Once formed, the lactase–alginate beads are stable at a neutral pH.

   a) Give two advantages of using immobilised enzymes in biotechnology.   [2 marks]

   b) Why is it important that the pH of the calcium alginate beads is neutral?   [2 marks]

   c) Apart from encapsulation, name another type of immobilisation.   [1 mark]

2. Home brewing typically uses a batch process. What must a brewer do to the equipment before setting up a new batch for brewing? Explain your answer.   [2 marks]

Ecosystems

An **ecosystem** is a community of all the living organisms in a given area that interact with the abiotic environment. Ecosystems vary in size and are dynamic. An ecosystem can be as small as a puddle or as large as a desert.

Changes to the biotic and abiotic components mean that the make up of an ecosystem changes over time.

Biotic Factors

The biotic factors are the living organisms in an ecosystem. They are classified into **autotrophs**, **heterotrophs**, **decomposers** and **detritivores**. The interactions of the different organisms alter the distribution of organisms in an ecosystem. Organisms can compete for resources (as competitors), cause disease (as pathogens), hunt prey (as predators), live off another organism while deriving nutrients at the host organism's expense (as parasites) or live in a symbiotic relationship where each derives benefit from the relationship.

Abiotic Factors

The abiotic factors are the physical and chemical non-living components of an ecosystem, i.e. the atmosphere, water and soil. They include factors such as pH, soil moisture, temperature, wind speed, light intensity and quality, precipitation, humidity, dissolved nutrients and salinity.

Food Chains

A food chain shows the way in which energy flows from producers (autotrophs) to consumers (heterotrophs).

Arrows indicate the direction that the energy flows:

Oak tree → caterpillar → great tit → sparrowhawk

Each position along the food chain is called a **trophic level**.

Biomass Transfer

Within an ecosystem there is a cycling of nutrients. Plants in the ecosystem synthesise organic compounds from atmospheric, or aquatic, carbon dioxide. Most of the sugars made are then used by the plant for respiration. The rest are used to make other organic compounds. These form the biomass of the plants. The biomass is then transferred to the organisms that feed on the plants.

Biomass can be measured either in terms of the mass of carbon in the organism or the dry mass of tissue per given area per given time.

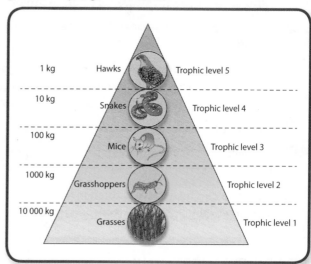

1 kg	Hawks	Trophic level 5
10 kg	Snakes	Trophic level 4
100 kg	Mice	Trophic level 3
1000 kg	Grasshoppers	Trophic level 2
10 000 kg	Grasses	Trophic level 1

Energy is lost at each trophic level and the available biomass decreases. The efficiency of biomass transfer also decreases each trophic level. This is because not all of the organic material is used in the consuming organism. For example, the mice will not turn all of the material in a grasshopper into material that makes a mouse. Not all of the grasshopper is eaten and not all the parts of a grasshopper are digestible.

The efficiency of biomass transfer is calculated by:

$$\text{Efficiency} = \frac{\text{Biomass transferred to the next level}}{\text{Total biomass in}} \times 100$$

In the food chain above the efficiency of biomass transfer from the grass to the grasshoppers is:

$$\text{Efficiency} = \frac{1000 \text{ kg}}{10\,000 \text{ kg}} \times 100 = 10\%$$

Gross primary production (GPP) is the chemical energy store in plant biomass in a given area or volume in a given time. Net primary production (NPP) is the chemical energy store in plant biomass after respiratory losses (R) to the environment have been taken into account.

This can be represented by NPP = GPP − R.

The net primary production is available for plant growth and reproduction. It is also available for other trophic levels, such as herbivores and decomposers.

The net production of consumers (N) can be calculated by taking I, the ingested chemical energy, food, F, the chemical energy lost to the environment in faeces and urine, and R, the respiratory losses to the environment.

This can be calculated as:

$N = I - (F + R)$

Human Manipulation

Humans have manipulated food chains to their own advantage for thousands of years. This is achieved through farming and hunting of organisms and by changing the biotic and abiotic factors. Resources, such as natural and artificial fertilisers, can be added to an ecosystem to increase the ecosystem's **carrying capacity**, to increase crop size or increase the number of animals present. Pests that would normally eat a crop are removed, diseases are cured and limiting factors, such as light levels and water availability, are increased. This simplifies food webs so energy losses to non-human food chains are reduced and reduces respiratory losses within a food chain ending with humans.

Not all action by farmers is positive. Excessive use of natural and artificial fertilisers can lead to leaching into nearby rivers and eutrophication. This is where excess nutrients cause a dense growth of algae and other aquatic plants. This leads to overcrowding and competition for sunlight, space and oxygen.

Recycling

The biomass of dead or decaying organisms is broken down by decomposers (saprobionts). This makes the organic material available for other organisms to utilise. Elements such as nitrogen and phosphorus are recycled. The organic matter is recycled repeatedly. The atoms that make up an organism will have been part of many other organisms and will continue to be so in the future.

Elements such as nitrogen and carbon are cycled through organisms and the ecosystem. Mycorrhizae are a symbiotic association between the roots of plants and fungi. These help uptake of water and inorganic ions by plants.

Nitrogen Cycle

Nitrogen makes up the majority of the Earth's atmosphere and is essential for living organisms as a constituent of DNA and protein. Atmospheric nitrogen is effectively inert, due to the presence of a triple covalent bond between nitrogen atoms.

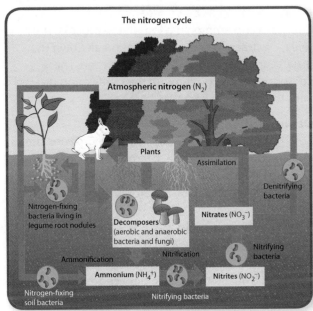

The nitrogen cycle

Nitrogen to Ammonia

Nitrogen-fixing bacteria such as *Azotobacter* and *Rhizobium* can fix atmospheric nitrogen into ammonia, which then gets converted into ammonium ions that can then be utilised by plants.

$$N_2 + 8H^+ + 8e^- \rightarrow 2NH_3 + H_2$$

Rhizobium bacteria can only fix nitrogen when they are inside root nodules of **legumes**. They invade the roots of a legume and then form a symbiotic relationship with the plant, providing ammonium ions and receiving amino acids in return from the plant.

Biological nitrogen fixation tends to be prevented by the presence of oxygen, so the microorganisms have to utilise proteins that protect the enzyme involved, nitrogenase, from oxygen.

Ammonia to Nitrite

Nitrifying bacteria of the genus *Nitrosomonas* can convert ammonium ions into nitrites (NO_2^-). They are found in areas that are high in nitrogen compounds, including soil and fresh water.

DAY 7

Nitrite to Nitrate
Nitrobacter is a genus of bacteria that oxidises nitrite into nitrate. This enables non-legumes to take up the nitrogen.

Decomposers
A variety of aerobic and anaerobic bacteria and fungi (saprobionts) break down organic material, releasing ammonia and ammonium ions in the process. They release extracellular enzymes that break down the organic molecules and are then absorbed. These compounds then go through the nitrification process with the nitrifying bacteria.

Denitrification
Some bacteria, such as *Thiobacillus denitrificans*, are able to convert nitrates back into diatomic nitrogen. This replenishes the nitrogen in the atmosphere. These bacteria respire by anaerobic respiration.

The Carbon Cycle
Carbon, like nitrogen, is essential for life on Earth. It is essential for all metabolic reactions in organisms. Carbon dioxide in the atmosphere currently forms 0.04% of the atmosphere, or 400 parts per million (ppm). Even though this may seem low, there is still ample to be used by all photosynthetic plants.

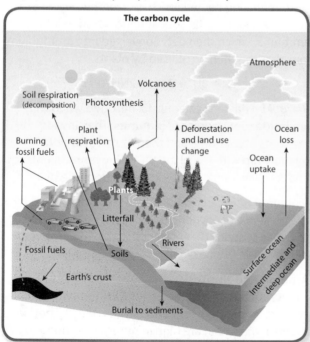

The carbon cycle

(b) act as carbon skeletons that can be used to make all other organic compounds in the body.

All living cells respire. Respiration releases carbon dioxide back into the atmosphere.

Decomposition
Decomposers break down the organic material. The carbon-containing compounds may be ingested and metabolised. Some of the carbon will be released through respiration as carbon dioxide.

Physical and Chemical Effects
When carbon is not in the atmosphere, it is said to be in a sink. Some carbon sinks can trap carbon for millions of years, e.g. fossil fuels. When the fossil fuel is released, it puts carbon back into the atmosphere. Forests also act as carbon sinks. If there is a forest fire, then the carbon that was originally fixed through photosynthesis will be released into the atmosphere as carbon dioxide through combustion.

Volcanoes and hot springs can also release large quantities of carbon dioxide. The heat causes the carbon dioxide to be produced from carbonates (e.g. limestone) that undergo thermal decomposition.

QUICK TEST

1. Define the term ecosystem.
2. What are abiotic factors?
3. What are biotic factors?
4. What does a food chain show?
5. What are trophic levels?
6. What is the formula for the efficiency of biomass transfer?
7. How have humans affected food chains?
8. Give the name of a type of nitrogen-fixing bacterium.
9. What species of bacteria convert ammonia into nitrite?
10. Why are coal and oil referred to as sinks of carbon?

Photosynthesis and Respiration
Photosynthesis is essential for life on Earth as the carbon compounds created (a) contain energy and

● An ecosystem is the community of all living organisms in a given area interacting with the abiotic environment. Ecosystems vary in size and are dynamic.

● Biotic factors include the autotrophs, heterotrophs, decomposers and detritivores. Competitors compete for resources. Pathogens cause disease. Predators hunt for prey. Parasites live off of other organisms.

● The abiotic factors are all of the non-living physical and chemical components of an ecosystem.

● Food chains show the direction of energy flow from the producers (autotrophs) to the consumers (heterotrophs).

● Cycling of nutrients occurs within an ecosystem.

● Each position on the food chain is a trophic level. The change in biomass can be measured for each trophic level of a food chain.

● The chemical energy store in plant biomass is called gross primary production (GPP). Net primary production (NPP) is the energy store after respiratory losses (R).

● The net production of consumers (N), such as animals, is calculated by taking the chemical energy in ingested food (I) and removing the losses due to faeces (F) and respiration (R).

● Humans have manipulated food chains for their own advantage for thousands of years through farming and hunting of organisms and by changing the biotic and abiotic factors.

● Recycling organic matter takes place through decomposers breaking down dead organisms.

● Elements such as nitrogen and carbon are cycled through organisms and the ecosystem.

● Nitrogen is effectively an inert gas due to its triple covalent bond. The gas is fixed into ammonia by nitrogen-fixing bacteria such as *Azotobacter* and *Rhizobium*.

● Ammonia is converted to nitrite (NO_2^-) by *Nitrosomonas* spp. Nitrite is converted to plant-friendly nitrate (NO_3^{2-}) by *Nitrobacter spp*.

● Decomposers break down organic matter into ammonia and ammonium ions (NH_4^+).

● The carbon cycle involves carbon in CO_2 gas being fixed by plants through photosynthesis. Respiration produces CO_2 gas as does decomposition by decomposers.

● When carbon is not in the atmosphere it is stored in a sink. Releasing the CO_2 from a sink occurs when fossil fuels are burned, volcanoes erupt and forest fires take place.

PRACTICE QUESTIONS

1. a) Name two molecules that contain nitrogen in living organisms.   [2 marks]

   b) What is the role of the following bacteria in the nitrogen cycle?

      Azotobacter

      Nitrosomonas

      Thiobacillus   [3 marks]

2. In 2016 the Paris Climate Agreement was signed by governments from around the world. One aim of the agreement was to reduce the amount of carbon dioxide in the atmosphere to limit the increase in global temperatures to less than 2°C. Explain how human activities have contributed to global warming.   [4 marks]

Population Size

The size of a population is dependent upon limiting factors, such as availability of food, space to live, temperature and availability of light (for plants). Any one of these can be the single limiting factor for population growth.

Carrying Capacity

The carrying capacity is the maximum size that a population can reach and sustain indefinitely in a particular habitat without significantly depleting or degrading the essential resources for that species. The essential resources include food, water and other factors.

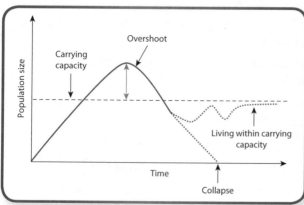

Predator–prey Relationships

The numbers of a predator and its prey follow a predictable relationship. As the number of prey increases, this leads to more predators as there are enough prey to support the larger population. This increase in predators leads, a little later, to a shortage of prey, which leads to a decrease in predator numbers, and so the cycle continues.

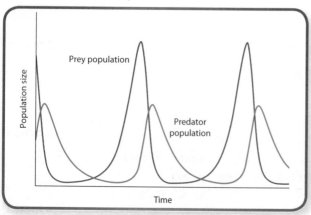

The numbers of prey do not generally collapse and reach zero as there are always pockets of prey that the predators cannot find and eat. Predation can therefore act as a strong agent of natural selection.

Competition

Competition for resources can be within a species (**intraspecific** competition) or between species (**interspecific** competition).

Gause's law of competitive exclusion states that two species competing for precisely the same resources cannot co-exist. Interspecific competition will lead to the eventual reduction in population size of one species.

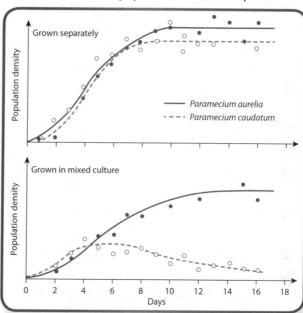

In this famous experiment two species of *Paramecium*, a genus of single-celled protozoans, are grown in flasks. *Paramecium caudatum* is larger than *Paramecium aurelia*. When they are both added to a flask with the same growth medium, after a period of days *P. aurelia* population growth continues while that of *P. caudatum* crashes. As they are competing for the same resource, it seems that being able to reproduce more quickly and having a larger surface area to volume ratio gives the smaller of the two species a competitive advantage.

Maintaining Biodiversity

It is important to maintain **biodiversity**. Resources from ecosystems include drugs, food and materials for manufacture. If biodiversity is reduced, then the availability of the resources decreases and may affect other parts of the food chain. Economically, this could prove extremely expensive. Managing the resources at hand would lead to cost savings in the future and potentially provide sources of drugs that reduce the load on the NHS. Socially there is a need to maintain biodiversity. People enjoy wildlife-related activities and this engagement satisfies people's desire to connect with each other and with nature. Even in cities, planners aim to include recreational spaces to allow people to come into contact with nature. Ethically it is not acceptable to wipe out all species deemed to be not useful to us. There is a general acceptance that humans are part of the global food chain and that humans are not separate from it. This means that there is in effect a duty of care as humans are the only organisms on the planet capable of understanding the consequences of our population growth and civilisation.

Conservation

Conservation involves managing natural resources sustainably. Areas that are conserved are managed. Resources can be removed but steps are taken to ensure they are also replaced or replenished. For example, many countries use timber for building materials. Forests are managed so that there is a cycle of cutting down mature trees for their timber and planting new stands of trees that will eventually be cut down themselves decades in the future. If the trees were not managed and tree-felling not followed by tree planting, there would be a loss of an ecosystem.

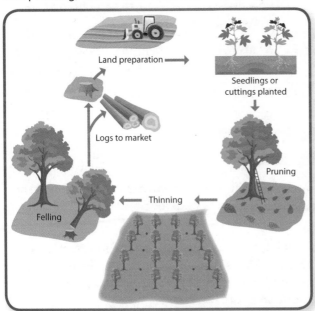

Commercial fishing can also be managed in a sustainable way. Quotas can be introduced to limit the amount of fish caught, ensuring that there are enough fish present that will grow to adulthood to maintain the necessary population size. There are restrictions on catching fish that are below a certain size, helping to keep enough fish that will survive to adulthood. Certain endangered fish are not allowed to be caught, with severe penalties for breaking the law.

The Masai Mara is a National Park in Kenya. It is a conservation area that is managed by the Kenyan Government. The animals and plants on the park are monitored and there is active involvement by vets and anti-poaching teams to ensure animals stay alive and healthy. Visitors can come to the park, their fees helping pay for the costs of conservation.

Preservation

Preservation differs from conservation by creating areas that are not managed or interfered with by humans. People are banned from entering areas that are preserved. This allows the ecosystem to be undisturbed. It protects rare and endangered plants and animals. These sites are visited only by scientists who monitor the populations.

Controlling Human Activities

In environmentally sensitive areas where there is a real risk of ecosystem destruction, management is needed to reduce the risk of human impact on the ecosystem. In the Galápagos Islands, off the coast of Ecuador, visitor numbers are restricted. Those that do visit can only move to defined areas. Checks are made to ensure that the visitors are not knowingly or unknowingly bringing in plant or animal material that could invade the islands. Close monitoring of visitors and restricting numbers help minimise the disturbance to conserved and preserved areas.

In the Snowdonia National Park in Wales there is a programme of building paths for walkers to walk on, minimising damage to vegetation. Some wetland areas of the park are preserved by the international **Ramsar Convention**, so people cannot enter them. By managing the park, people can come and visit an area of outstanding beauty while ecosystems are being preserved.

Succession

Succession is the term given to the colonisation of land by living organisms. The first organisms to colonise barren rock are typically lichens (a symbiosis between bacteria and fungi) and mosses. Multicellular plants require soil, so there has to be some erosion before the first **pioneer species** can grow. The lichen alters the rock and helps with erosion, creating soil.

The pioneer species alter the habitat themselves, making it more suitable for the next tier of organisms. As they grow, they trap water and change the habitat, which enables other species to start to grow. This process continues until the land can support the growth of forests. This is called the climax community.

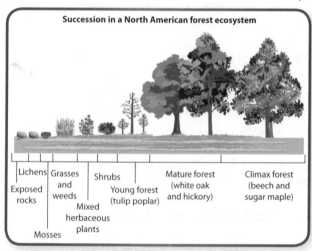

Succession in a North American forest ecosystem

| Lichens | Grasses and weeds | Shrubs | Mature forest (white oak and hickory) | Climax forest (beech and sugar maple) |

Exposed rocks — Mosses — Mixed herbaceous plants — Young forest (tulip poplar)

Succession can also occur when there is a forest fire, leading to an ecosystem starting again.

If there is no soil present then it is called primary succession. If there is soil present, e.g. after a forest fire, then it is secondary succession.

Deflected Succession

The actions of humans can alter the natural progression of succession. Many areas that are thought of as being natural are actually managed. Areas covered in grassland are maintained by introducing animals, such as sheep and cows, that prevent shrub and tree growth. This is **deflected succession**. If the herbivores were removed, the succession would continue and climax forest would eventually grow. In the UK, England was covered with a very large forest up until the time of Henry VIII. Due to tree-felling to provide timber for the Royal Navy, the majority of the forest was cut down.

QUICK TEST

1. What is the carrying capacity of a population?

2. Describe the relationship between predator and prey.

3. Why will the prey normally never completely die out?

4. What are intra- and interspecific competition?

5. State Gause's law of competitive exclusion.

6. Why is it important to maintain biodiversity?

7. How would a woodland used for logging be conserved?

8. How does a preserved area differ from a conserved one?

9. What are the first organisms to colonise newly formed volcanic rock?

10. What is deflected succession?

SUMMARY

- The carrying capacity of a population is the maximum size that a population can reach and sustain indefinitely without depleting or degrading the essential resources (e.g. food and water) for that species in a habitat.

- The numbers of predators and their prey follow a predictable relationship. As the number of prey increases, the number of predators will increase. This decreases the number of prey which then leads to a decrease in the number of predators. The number of prey should never collapse as there will always be pockets surviving that escape the attention of the predators.

- Competition for resources can be intra- or interspecific. Intraspecific competition is where members of the same species compete with each other for resources. Interspecific competition is where more than one species compete for the same resources.

- Gause's law of competitive exclusion states that two species competing for the same resources cannot co-exist. So, when resources are in short supply only one of the competing species will survive.

- This can be shown experimentally with *Paramecium* species surviving in separate culture medium. When mixed together, the species that can breed the fastest and grow the quickest ends up taking over the medium.

- Biodiversity is the range and genetic diversity of organisms in an ecosystem.

- Humans get a lot of resources from the ecosystem, e.g. drugs, food and materials for manufacture. Reducing biodiversity may lead to the loss of undiscovered drugs, foods and materials.

- People also require wildlife-related activities and the satisfaction of interacting with the natural world.

- There is effectively a duty of care to prevent ecosystem destruction as humans are the only organisms capable of understanding the consequences of destroying it.

- Conservation involves managing natural resources sustainably, replacing and regrowing resources. Trees being felled in conserved woodland are replanted to ensure there is a continual supply. Fishing quotas can be introduced, with size limits to catches, as well as captive breeding programmes.

- Preservation is where an area is not managed or interfered with by humans (other than by monitoring), enabling ecosystems to be undisturbed, protecting rare habitats and organisms.

- Succession is where an area is colonised by pioneer plants and animals over time.

- As bare rock is colonised, this enables soil to form which leads to more advanced plants. Eventually this leads to climax communities of forests to grow.

- Deflected succession is where humans alter the land, preventing progression to climax woodland. Sheep and cows grazing on grass, preventing shrub and forest formation are examples.

PRACTICE QUESTIONS

1. Sumatran tigers are the smallest surviving tiger subspecies. They are distinguished by heavy black stripes on their orange coats.

   The Sumatran tiger lives in forests on the island of Sumatra. The most recent estimates from the World Wide Fund for Nature are that there are around 300 individual tigers left on Sumatra. They are critically endangered.

   a) i) Suggest what is meant by the term critically endangered. **[1 mark]**

   ii) Give two reasons why the Sumatran tiger is critically endangered. **[2 marks]**

   b) In an effort to save the Sumatran tiger, a global captive breeding programme has been set up. This unites five regional zoo organisations across Europe, America, Australia, Japan and Indonesia. The programme has 375 tigers.

   Explain why the tigers are being conserved in captivity (*ex situ*) rather than in the wild (*in situ*). **[3 marks]**

Answers

DAY 1

Cell Signalling
QUICK TEST (Page 7)

1. Gradients enable a cell or organism to determine the direction of the source of a stimulus.
2. Cell recognition is the ability of cells to recognise each other via direct or indirect contact.
3. A connexon is a transmembrane protein that connects to an adjacent cell, creating a pore that hydrophilic substances can move through.
4. Glycoproteins and glycolipids.
5. Water-loving.
6. Plasmodesmata are the plant equivalent of connexons. They extend into the plant cell wall.
7. Diagram showing cells separated by a short distance being influenced by other cells. For example:

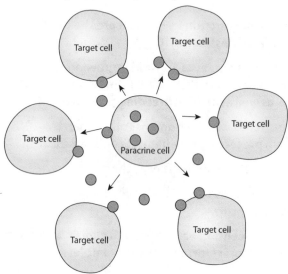

8. Synaptic signalling is where a neurone releases a neurotransmitter into a synapse. The neurotransmitter then stimulates a response in the receiving cell, e.g. an effector cell, or another neurone.
9. Endocrine signalling can operate over a much larger distance.
10. Plant growth regulators are substances that are produced in special cells that then have an effect elsewhere in the plant.

PRACTICE QUESTIONS (Page 7)

1. a) Animal cells possess transmembrane proteins, called connexons, connecting the interior of a cell to the outside [1]. Connexons connect to the corresponding connexon on another cell [1].
   b) Plasmodesmata in plant cell walls are used to send signals between cells [1]; they allow hydrophilic substances to move between cells [1].
   c) All life must come from a common ancestor [1].

2. a) Paracrine signalling is where signalling chemicals pass to local cells, e.g. regulator chemicals such as growth factors in the space between cells [1]. Synaptic signalling is where a signalling substance (a neurotransmitter) is transported in a cell and then crosses a gap between nerve cells (the synapse) [1]. The paracrine signals are not for a specific cell [1] whereas the synaptic signal is [1].
   b) Endocrine signalling is where signals can be sent over a long distance [1] and only affect cells with target proteins on their cell surface membrane [1].

Homeostasis
QUICK TEST (Page 10)

1. Homeostasis is the maintenance of a constant internal body environment.
2. Three from: temperature/thermal; pH; fluid; glucose; ions; calcium.
3. The brain.
4. Muscles and glands.
5. Negative feedback is where the body responds to a change in a stimulus by acting to reverse it.
6. Whereas negative feedback acts to reduce the effect of a change, positive feedback causes the stimulus to increase further.
7. Oxytocin causes contractions to occur. The contractions themselves cause more oxytocin to be released, which cause increased frequency and strength of contractions, which releases more oxytocin.
8. Endotherms generate body heat from metabolism. Ectotherms do not generate enough heat from metabolism and so need to find environmental sources of heat to warm their bodies.
9. If temperature gets too low, then impulses from the hypothalamus cause muscle effectors to raise body hair, creating a layer of air around the body, and muscles to contract and relax, causing shivering. Shunt vessels on arterioles leading to capillary beds near the skin surface are closed, causing the blood to flow more deeply, reducing heat loss from the skin.
10. Generating body heat from metabolic reactions requires a lot of energy from food. Ectotherms do not generate body heat in this way, so they need less energy.

PRACTICE QUESTIONS (Page 11)

1. a) Thermoregulation/temperature homeostasis [1].
   b) The opah would be faster [1] to hunt prey [1] and able to dive to colder, deeper depths [1] and stay there without having to move up to warmer water [1].
   [2 marks: 1 mark for each point made]
   c) Enzymes will be denatured at temperatures 40°C and higher [1].

Excretion

QUICK TEST (Page 14)

1. Waste products cannot be used or stored safely.
2. Egestion is the removal of non-digested material from the body; excretion is the removal of waste.
3. $C_6H_{12}O_6 + 6O_2 \rightarrow 6H_2O + 6CO_2$
4. False.
5. Amino acids.
6. 2CROCOOH + 2NH$_3$; carboxylic acid and ammonia.
7. Carbon dioxide and ammonia.
8. Hepatic artery and hepatic portal vein.
9. Hepatocytes.
10. Glycogen.

PRACTICE QUESTIONS (Page 15)

1. a) i) Hepatic portal vein [1] and hepatic artery [1].
      ii) Inferior vena cava [1].
   b)

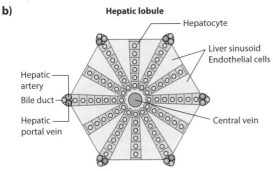

Hepatic lobule

Any six from: hexagonal shape [1]; central vein shown [1]; hepatocytes radiate outward [1]; bile duct [1]; (interlobular) vein [1]; and (interlobular) artery shown [1]; grouped together in groups of three [1]. **[6 marks: 1 mark for each point made]**

   c) $CO_2 + 2NH_3 \rightarrow (NH_2)_2CO + H_2O$ **[2 marks: 1 mark for left hand side; 1 mark for right hand side]**

The Kidney

QUICK TEST (Page 19)

1. Reptiles, birds, mammals.
2. Ureter takes urine from the kidney to the bladder; urethra takes it from the bladder to be removed form the body.
3. In the Bowman's capsule.
4. Increase surface area to volume ratio.
5. Hydrogen and bicarbonate ions.
6. The thick ascending loop reabsorbs ions via active transport.
7. Counter-current flow.
8. The hypothalamus responds by sending a signal to the posterior pituitary gland to decrease production of ADH.
9. ADH opens aquaporin proteins in the collecting duct and distal convoluted tubule, allowing water to flow back into the blood.
10. The urine will be dilute/large volume.

PRACTICE QUESTIONS (Page 19)

1. a) X = ureter [1], Y = medulla [1], Z = cortex [1].
   b) The nephron is the functional unit of the kidney [1] where blood is filtered and key molecules removed to form urine [1] and other molecules are reabsorbed when needed [1].
   c) i) The glomerulus is the part of the nephron where the blood is filtered [1]. It is a capillary bed with a large surface area for the movement of substances at high pressure [1].
      ii) The loop of Henle is a U-shaped structure found in the renal medulla [1]. Its function is to reabsorb water and important ions, such as sodium, potassium and chloride ions [1].

DAY 2

Nervous Communication

QUICK TEST (Page 22)

1. 1–120 m/s.
2. The central nervous system (CNS) and peripheral nervous system (PNS).
3. Mechanoreceptors detect pressure changes, nociceptors detect pain and proprioceptors detect changes in position.
4. Three from thermoreceptors, electromagnetic receptors, chemoreceptors, baroreceptors and osmoreceptors.
5. Conversion of a stimulus to an electrical signal or of an electrical signal to a physical action.
6. Muscle and gland.
7.

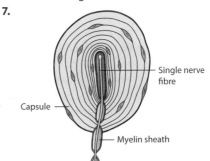

8. Sensory, relay and effector (motor).
9. Nodes of Ranvier are gaps appearing in the myelinated sheath of neurones every 1–3 mm.
10. Rhodopsin changes shape to form activated rhodopsin.

PRACTICE QUESTIONS (Page 23)

1. a) X = capsule [1], Y = myelin sheath [1], Z = nerve fibre [1].
   b) It is a mechanoreceptor [1].
   c) **Any three from:** the function of myelination is to speed up nerve impulses; this is because the receptor is detecting pressure changes; and it is important to act on these rapidly; otherwise damage may occur to the body **[3 marks: 1 mark for each point made]**.

Electrical Signals

QUICK TEST (Page 27)

1. A difference in charge between the inside of the axon and the outside.
2. −70 mV.
3. −55 mV.
4. 3 Na^+ to 2 K^+.
5. A stimulus causes voltage-gated Na^+ channels to open and the sodium ions move inwards down their concentration gradient.
6. Voltage-gated K^+ channels open, allowing K^+ to move out of the neurone down their concentration gradient.
7. There is a delay before the voltage-gated K^+ channels close.
8. The refractory period is the time during which the neurone cannot be restimulated.
9. Acetylcholine.
10. 100 potentials per second.

PRACTICE QUESTIONS (Page 27)

1. a) The acetylcholine crosses the synapse and attaches to special channel proteins, changing their shape [1]. This allows sodium ions to pass through the membrane, causing depolarisation/reducing the potential difference [1]. Once the potential reaches a particular value in the next axon an action potential is initiated [1].

    b) **Any two from:** if the neurotransmitter remained then it would keep binding to the channel proteins and further impulses would not be able to be sent [1]. Depolarisation of the postsynaptic membrane would be continuous [1]. **[2 marks: 1 mark for each point made]**

    c) **Any two from:** the diaphragm is a muscle [1]. If sarin binds to the protein that breaks up acetylcholine, the amount of the neurotransmitter would not drop [1]. This would mean that the person inhaling the gas would not be able to contract their diaphragm [1] so they would suffocate [1]. **[2 marks: 1 mark for each point made]**

Endocrine System

QUICK TEST (Page 29)

1. Via hormones secreted directly into blood.
2. At the top of each kidney.
3. Three from: pineal, hypothalamus, pituitary, thyroid, thymus, parathyroid, pancreas, ovary, testis.
4. The endocrine gland is ductless whereas exocrine glands have a duct.
5. A receptor specific to that hormone.
6. The adrenal medulla.
7. Cortisol and aldosterone.
8. Acinar cells or acini.
9. Alpha and beta cells.
10. Glucagon and insulin.

PRACTICE QUESTIONS (Page 31)

1. a) i) R [1]
       ii) Q [1]

    b) The pancreas produces insulin when glucose levels are high [1] and glucagon when glucose levels are low [1] as well as pancreatic amylase for digestion [1].

    c) X = intralobular duct [1], Y = islets of Langerhans [1], Z = acinar cells or acini [1].

Control of Blood Glucose

QUICK TEST (Page 35)

1. The glucose can cause kidney, nerve and cardiovascular damage as well as blindness.
2. Liver, muscle and fat cells.
3. Their blood sugar level is too low.
4. Potassium/K^+ and calcium/Ca^{2+}.
5. GLUT2.
6. GLUT4.
7. Glucagon suppresses insulin and causes the liver to convert glycogen back into glucose.
8. Type II diabetes is where the islets of Langerhans are put under too much pressure due to desensitisation of the liver, muscle and fat cells to glucose. Type I is caused by the immune system attacking and destroying the beta cells.
9. Through diet, exercise and medicinal drugs.
10. Stem cells may be used to replace the faulty cells in the pancreas. An artificial pancreas may be built.

PRACTICE QUESTIONS (Page 35)

1. a) **Any two from:** type I diabetes is caused by the immune system; which is often triggered by a viral infection; leading to the destruction of the beta cells in the islets of Langerhans in the pancreas; the beta cells produce insulin, so if they are killed no insulin is made; in some cases this is inherited. **[2 marks: 1 mark for each point made]**

    b) **Any six from:** after food is eaten beta cells in the islets of Langerhans in the pancreas [1] are signalled to release insulin into the blood [1]. The insulin moves to the liver, muscle and fat cells [1]. Insulin binds to a receptor [1], initiating the insulin signalling pathway [1]. This allows the GLUT4 receptor to pass glucose into the cell [1]. High levels of glucose in the liver are then converted into glycogen [1]. Glucagon is produced by the alpha cells [1] when glucose levels in the body drop [1] and it suppresses insulin production [1]. The glucagon is transported to liver and muscle cells [1] where it triggers the breakdown of glycogen into glucose [1]. **[6 marks: 1 mark for each point made]**

    c) **Any three from:** the symptoms can be mistaken for other things; people don't visit the doctor often enough; people aren't having the blood tests for the condition; lack of awareness of the condition and the consequences; the symptoms are not dangerous until the condition is quite far progressed. **[3 marks: 1 mark for each point made]**

Plant Growth Regulators

QUICK TEST (Page 39)

1. Biotic factors are caused by living things; abiotic factors relate to the non-living environment.
2. Abiotic factors.
3. Phototropism: grows towards or away from light. Chemotropism: grows towards or away from chemicals.
4. Three from: geotropism (gravitropism), heliotropism, thermotropism, thigmotropism.
5. They can repel it or poison it.
6. Amino acids.
7. Plant growth regulators/plant hormones.
8. Auxin makes the cells at the abscission site less susceptible to another PGR, ethylene. When auxin levels decline, ethylene causes enzymes to break down cell walls at the abscission site, causing the leaves to drop.
9. ABA prevents germination. When it is time to germinate, ABA levels drop and gibberellins increase, which leads to germination.
10. Gibberellin causes stem elongation.

PRACTICE QUESTIONS (Page 39)

1. a) i) A plant growth regulator/plant hormone [1].
      ii) Rate of growth $= \dfrac{\text{Value at day 6} - \text{Value at day 3}}{3}$
         $= \dfrac{62 - 6}{3}$
         $= 18.7$ mm/day
         [2 marks: 1 mark for correct answer; 1 mark for correct working. Only award 1 mark for: correct answer on its own; incorrect answer with working within ±1; answer not to 3 s.f.]
   b) **Any four from:** The concentration of gibberellin increases then decreases; while the length of the hypocotyls increases initially slowly then more rapidly before levelling off; this is because gibberellins increase the length of the hypocotyls; by causing cell elongation; when gibberellin levels decrease, the hypocotyls stop growing; this is when the cotyledons become green/the plant starts photosynthesising.
      [4 marks: 1 mark for each point made]

Plant Experiments

QUICK TEST (Page 43)

1. No ethical considerations, plants are easy to grow and plants do not move around.
2. Charles Darwin.
3. The coleoptile.
4. Blocking the movement of the chemical with a mica plate and replacing the coleoptile in a different position.
5. Agar blocks.
6. Auxin/indole-3-acectic acid/IAA.
7. A clinostat.
8. In the presence of auxin, growth in root cells is inhibited.
9. Remove the apex and see how it affects the side shoots.
10. Fruit ripening, rooting powders for cuttings and weedkillers.

PRACTICE QUESTIONS (Page 43)

1. a) Gravitropism/geotropism [1].
   b) In the root IAA inhibits growth [1] so the cells on the upper surface elongate more due to the lower concentration of IAA in that area, causing the root to bend downwards [1].
   c)

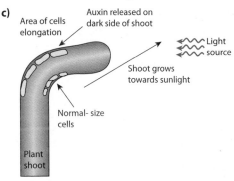

   [2 marks: 1 mark for diagram with a curvature to the right; 1 mark for auxin present on the side furthest from the light source]

DAY 3

Nervous System Organisation

QUICK TEST (Page 47)

1. Into the autonomic and somatic nervous systems.
2. Autonomic.
3. On the outer layer of the brain.
4. Muscular activity (balance and movement), learning and remembering motor skills.
5. It is a continuation of the spinal cord, at the base of the brain.
6. It controls the heart and lungs (pulse and breathing rates).
7. It is a pea-sized gland at the base of the hypothalamus.
8. Neurohormones.
9. Detection of a stimulus, sensory neurone signals a relay neurone in the spine, response is sent via an effector (motor) neurone to the effector and the effector carries out the response.
10. It controls growth, blood pressure, the thyroid gland and metabolism.

PRACTICE QUESTIONS (Page 47)

1. a) Muscles and glands are types of effector [1]; they carry out the response of the reflex action [1].
   b) i) W = white matter [1], X = grey matter [1], Y = sensory neurone [1], Z = motor or effector neurone [1].
      ii) White matter contains the myelinated neurones [1] that receive messages from receptors and send the response to the effectors [1]. Grey matter is made up of unmyelinated cells [1] and coordinates the response [1].

c) Reflexes allow an involuntary, near-instantaneous response **[1]** to a potentially life-threatening stimulus **[1]**.

Muscle Action

QUICK TEST (Page 50)

1. Adrenocorticotropic hormone (ACTH).
2. The adrenal glands.
3. It is a hormone that triggers a number of other hormones.
4. Cyclic AMP.
5. It activates a protein kinase, which triggers the breakdown of glycogen into glucose.
6. Involuntary (smooth) muscle.
7. Bundles of muscle fibres.
8. Actin and myosin.
9. Its role is to maintain levels of ATP.
10. The intercalated discs enable electrical impulses to be sent rapidly throughout the heart, coordinating contractions.

PRACTICE QUESTIONS (Page 51)

1. **a)** B **[1]**
   b) A fascicle **[1]**.
   c) Levels of ATP are high inside the mitochondria, whereas levels of creatine phosphate are low **[1]**. The conversion of ATP to creatine phosphate is favoured **[1]**. The creatine phosphate diffuses from the mitochondria to the myofibril **[1]**. Once in the myofibril, the level of ADP is high when the myofibril is contracted, so creatine phosphate is converted back into ATP **[1]**.

Skeletal Tissues

QUICK TEST (Page 54)

1. Cartilage is a flexible connective tissue; it is stiffer and less flexible than muscle but not as rigid as bone.
2. Hyaline cartilage.
3. White fibrous cartilage.
4. Collagen and chondrocytes.
5. Its role is to surround and enclose the cartilage.
6. White fibrous cartilage.
7. Compact bone and cancellous bone.
8. It is a material consisting of calcium and phosphate, giving bone its rigidity.
9. Osteoblasts make new bone; osteoclasts break down bone.
10. Reabsorption of calcium from the bone.

PRACTICE QUESTIONS (Page 55)

1. **a)** **Any two from:** pain across the whole body; muscle weakness; bone fragility. **[2 marks: 1 mark for each point made]**
   b) Lack of calcium in the diet **[1]**. Lack of vitamin D **[1]**.
   c) **Any two from:** hydroxyapatite is formed from calcium; and phosphate; the calcium is taken away, which means that 70% of the bone breaks down; the bones are more likely to fracture. **[2 marks: 1 mark for each point made]**

d) X = Haversian canal **[1]**, Y = osteocyte **[1]**, Z = canaliculi **[1]**.

e) Rickets **[1]**.

Any three from: it is more severe because the bones are still developing/adult bones have already developed; so the bones will have defective calcification; causing bones to bow. **[3 marks: 1 mark for each point made]**

The Skeleton

QUICK TEST (Page 58)

1. The appendicular skeleton.
2. A displaced fracture.
3. In an open fracture the bone breaks through the skin, exposing it to pathogens and infection.
4. The function is to enclose and protect the spinal cord while allowing for movement.
5. Cervical, thoracic, lumbar and sacrum.
6. The five lumbar vertebrae.
7. Scoliosis is where the spine curves laterally, caused by accident or abnormal muscle or nerves.
8. A child's skeleton is still growing.
9. The thoracic vertebrae become excessively curved (a hunched back) due to the front part of the vertebrae collapsing.
10. (a) Condyloid; (b) hinge.

PRACTICE QUESTIONS (Page 59)

1. **a)** W = cervical vertebrae **[1]**, X = thoracic vertebrae **[1]**, Y = lumbar vertebrae **[1]**, Z = sacrum **[1]**.

   b)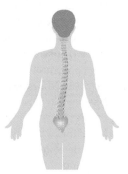

   Diagram with spine **[1]** showing a clear bend to left or right **[1]**, as shown.

   c) **Any two from:** back brace; (surgery) inserting metal rods; (surgery) fusing vertebrae together. **[2 marks: 1 mark for each point made]**

DAY 4
Photosynthesis
QUICK TEST (Page 62)
1. Inside the chloroplast.
2. The stroma is the liquid filling the inside of the chloroplast.
3.
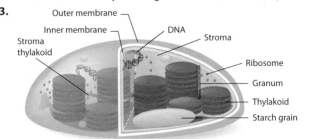

4. Blue (425–450 nm) and red (600–700 nm).
5. Chlorophylls and carotenoid pigments.
6. PSII.
7. Photons excite chlorophyll in the PSII complex and drive the breakdown of water to form O_2 and H^+ ions.
8. Two.
9. $NADPH_2$.
10. ATP synthase.

PRACTICE QUESTIONS (Page 63)
1. a) DCMU would prevent the electrons from progressing from plastoquinone to cytochrome [1] and on to plastocyanin [1].
   b) There would be no electrons passed to PSI [1], so no NADPH would be formed [1].

Light-Independent Stage
QUICK TEST (Page 65)
1. The light-independent reactions depend on the products of light-dependent reactions not affected by light.
2. The Calvin cycle.
3. RuBP.
4. Rubisco.
5. A triose phosphate.
6. Two G3P molecules.
7. Two from: light, carbon dioxide, temperature.
8. At each stage an enzyme catalyses the conversion of one reactant to another product which becomes the next reactant in the sequence.
9. They can stop the enzyme or slow them down, preventing the cycle from progressing.
10. Water is required for photosynthesis so the reaction would stop due to a lack of this reactant.

PRACTICE QUESTIONS (Page 67)
1. a) Carbon dioxide/CO_2 [1].
   b) The light-independent stage [1].
   c) ATP [1] and NADPH [1].
   d) P [1] and S [1].
   e) Ribulose bisphosphate carboxylase oxygenase/Rubisco [1].

Respiration
QUICK TEST (Page 71)
1. Respiration is the process in which energy stored in complex molecules is transferred to ATP.
2. Mitochondrion/mitochondria.
3.
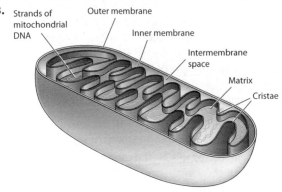

4. ATP, ADP, ions and nutrients all pass easily through the membrane.
5. The cristae increase the surface area of the inner membrane for diffusion and to allow the presence of more transport proteins.
6. The matrix contains enzymes involved in the Krebs cycle (or the citric acid cycle) as well as dissolved O_2, H_2O, CO_2 and the various intermediates for the reactions.
7. Glycolysis, link reaction, Krebs cycle and oxidative phosphorylation/electron transport chain.
8. Two molecules of CO_2, three molecules of NADH and one molecule of $FADH_2$ are produced from every turn of the cycle.
9. Oxidative phosphorylation is the final stage of respiration where electrons are fed into the electron transport chain to ultimately generate ATP.
10. ATP synthase.

PRACTICE QUESTIONS (Page 71)
1. a) i) X = glycolysis [1], Y = link reaction [1], Z = Krebs cycle [1].
      ii) In the matrix of the mitochondrion [1].
      iii) FAD (accept $FADH_2$) [1].
   b) Decarboxylation is the removal of carbon dioxide/carboxyl group [1].
   c) Anaerobic respiration [1].

Holoenzymes
QUICK TEST (Page 74)
1. Lower it.
2. The apoenzyme does not have a cofactor bound to it.
3. Coenzymes are substrates in the reaction and are altered as a result.
4. Coenzymes transport chemical groups between the different enzymes in a metabolic pathway.
5. $NAD^+ + 2H^+ + 2e^- \rightarrow NADH + H^+$.
6. Pyruvate.

7. Aerobic respiration produces:
   a) 6–8 ATP from glycolysis (2 ATP + the oxidative phosphorylation of 2 NADH)
   b) 6 ATP from the oxidation of pyruvate (the oxidative phosphorylation of 2 NADH)
   c) 24 ATP from the Krebs cycle (2 ATP + the oxidative phosphorylation of 6 NADH and 2 FADH$_2$).
8. Anaerobic respiration produces 2 ATP, so 19 times inefficient (based on predicted 38 ATP).
9. Pyruvate + NADH $\rightarrow$ NAD$^+$ + lactate; Lactate + H$^+$ $\rightleftharpoons$ lactic acid.
10. Mammals lack the enzyme alcohol dehydrogenase.

PRACTICE QUESTIONS (Page 75)

1. Pyruvate reacts with NADH to form NAD$^+$ and lactate [1]. This is then reacted with H$^+$ and converted to lactic acid [1]. (Also accept equations:
   Pyruvate + NADH $\rightarrow$ NAD$^+$ + lactate [1]
   Lactate + H$^+$ $\rightleftharpoons$ lactic acid [1])
2. a) RQ is a measure of the ratio of carbon dioxide given out to the oxygen consumed by an organism over a given period [1].
   b) **Any six from:** seeds soaked in water have a low amount of respiration [1]; carbohydrates in the seed are being used for that respiration [1]. Seeds after 12 hours in the soil have more oxygen compared to the water-soaked seeds [1], The seed will be using fat stores for aerobic respiration [1]. Seeds after 25 days are photosynthesising [1], carrying out aerobic respiration [1] using carbohydrates as a substrate [1]. [6 marks: 1 mark for each point made]

DAY 5

Mutations
QUICK TEST (Page 79)

1. An insertion mutation is where one or more nucleotides are inserted into a DNA sequence.
2. In a substitution mutation one or more nucleotides are replaced by other nucleotides.
3. In a deletion mutation one or more nucleotides are removed from a DNA sequence, shortening it.
4. Beneficial, neutral or harmful.
5. There is redundancy in the genetic code with more than one triplet code coding for an amino acid.
6. A nucleotide substitution would have the most impact at the start of the triplet code, in the first position.
7. The protein formed would need to be more effective at its role or confer a new use that benefits the organism.
8. All metabolic reactions involve enzymes, coded for by genes. If the enzymes are altered the reactions will not take place or will be faster or slower, depending on whether they are beneficial or harmful.

9. The cell with the mutation for a process at the start of a metabolic reaction is more likely to be adversely affected.
10. Although harmful, they may confer an advantage to those who carry the mutation, e.g. mutations that cause cystic fibrosis help a carrier to survive cholera.

PRACTICE QUESTIONS (Page 79)

1. a) **Any two from:** this is an insertion mutation; of two base pairs GG; causing a frameshift. [2 marks: 1 mark for each point made]
   b) **Any two from:** this is a deletion mutation; of four base pairs GTGT; causing a frameshift. [2 marks: 1 mark for each point made]
   c) The combined mutations would have altered the sequences of amino acids [1], changing the shape of the protein/taste receptor [1], so that it no longer was able to detect umami [1].
   d) The failure of the umami taste receptor [1] made eating meat taste bland/eating bamboo was tastier [1].

Regulatory Mechanisms
QUICK TEST (Page 83)

1. An operon is a unit of DNA containing a cluster of genes controlled by a single promoter.
2. When it receives a signal that the genes under the control of the operon are not needed.
3. A repressor protein.
4. It binds to the operator section of the operon and prevents transcription from taking place.
5. It functions in the absence of lactose.
6. In eukaryotes transcription factors exist that allow more than one protein to be produced from one gene.
7. A transcription factor is a protein that binds to specific DNA sequences and controls the rate of transcription.
8. Exons consist of the DNA that codes for a protein; introns do not.
9. Pre-mRNA contains exons and introns; mRNA contains only exons.
10. Post-translational modification involves prosthetic groups being added to a protein, altering its properties.

PRACTICE QUESTIONS (Page 83)

1. a) W = regulator gene [1], X = promoter [1], Y = operator [1].
   b) In the absence of lactose [1].
   c) **Any four from:** when lactose is absent, the regulator gene is transcribed, forming mRNA; this is then translated into a regulatory protein; the regulatory protein binds to the operon; this prevents RNA polymerase; from transcribing the structural genes for lactase. [4 marks: 1 mark for each point made]

Embryonic Development

QUICK TEST (Page 87)

1. The genes in animals are very similar to those in plants and fungi.
2. They control genes regulating cell differentiation and the development of the anatomy.
3. Homeodomain proteins.
4. The organism would not develop.
5. 235 active homeoboxes and 65 which do not code for proteins.
6. Hox genes are the homeobox genes concerned with the development of embryonic regions from head to tail.
7. The order that the Hox genes appear is the same as where the organs and appendages appear on the body.
8. Controlled/programmed cell death.
9. To ensure that only the target cell is affected.
10. Mitochondria.

PRACTICE QUESTIONS (Page 87)

1. a) All cells carry the genetic code to make an entire organism [1].
   b) **Any two from:** it is a regulatory gene; containing 180 base pairs/coding for 60 amino acids; controls the body development/body plan; codes for a gene product that binds to DNA; initiates transcription/switches genes on and off. [2 marks: 1 mark for each point made]
   c) Plants or fungi [1].
   d) **Any two from:** the genes are extremely important; mutations can affect the body plan/lead to parts developing in the wrong place; would be knock-on effects/consequences; mutation very likely to be lethal. [2 marks: 1 mark for each point made]
   e) All life evolved from a common ancestor/plants, animals and fungi share a common ancestor [1].

Inheritance

QUICK TEST (Page 90)

1. Having two copies of each chromosome.
2. Gg.
3. 1 in 4/25%.
4. Dihybrid inheritance is where a condition is controlled by two genes that are not linked and on separate chromosomes.
5. The number of alleles must be more than two.
6. Codominance is where neither of a pair of alleles is dominant to the other so both are expressed, giving a third phenotype.
7. I^AI^A Group A
   I^Ai Group A
   I^BI^B Group B
   I^Bi Group B
   I^AI^B Group AB
   ii Group O
8. Males.

9. Females have two X chromosomes so would have an alternative that may carry the dominant allele. Males carry only one X chromosome. If it has the recessive trait, they will definitely have the condition.
10. It will not affect female offspring.

PRACTICE QUESTIONS (Page 91)

1. a) Mothers 2/5 have vitamin D-resistant rickets but at least one offspring that does not [1]; this means that each mother must be heterozygous/a carrier [1]. Alternative answer: offspring 4/7 and 8 do not have vitamin D-resistant rickets but their parents do [1] so the mother must be heterozygous/a carrier [1]. [2 marks: 1 mark for each point made]
   b) It is sex linked because males without vitamin D-resistant rickets have fathers who do have the condition/4 does not have the condition but 1 has vitamin D-resistant rickets/7 and/or 8 does not have rickets but 6 has vitamin D-resistant rickets [1].
   c)

	X^R	X^r
X^R	X^RX^R Vitamin D resistant	X^RX^r Vitamin D resistant
Y	X^RY Vitamin D resistant	X^rY No vitamin D resistance

   0.25/1 in 4/25% chance [1] [4 marks: 1 mark for parental genotypes; 1 mark for offspring; 1 mark phenotypes]

DAY 6

Variation

QUICK TEST (Page 94)

1. Continuous variation.
2. Discontinuous variation.
3. Stabilising selection.
4.

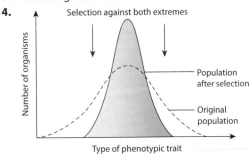

5. Neck length of giraffe.
6. There is positive selection for individuals possessing a particular trait. Over time it becomes the norm for the population; the less beneficial trait is selected against.

7.

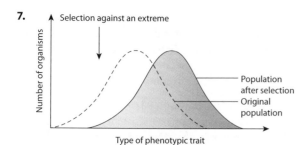

Selection against an extreme

Number of organisms ↑

Population after selection

Original population

Type of phenotypic trait →

8. Genetic drift is a basic, random process leading to a change in frequency of an allele.

9. Genetic bottleneck.

10. Allopatric speciation is where species get separated into geographically isolated populations that cannot breed whereas sympatric speciation is where new species evolve in the same geographic region, in which a new behaviour may mean members of the same species can no longer come together to mate.

PRACTICE QUESTIONS (Page 95)

1. a) i) A genetic bottleneck is where there has been a sharp reduction in the size of a population due to a significant environmental change **[1]**.

    ii) **Any two from:** the population on Guadalupe will have a smaller range of alleles/traits; and most of the population will share the same traits/alleles; this means that they are likely to be more affected by further environmental change/will not be able to adapt to environmental change; they will be susceptible to inbreeding and recessive disorders.
    [2 marks: 1 mark for each point made]

  b) The founder effect **[1]**.

  c) Allopatric speciation **[1]**.

Analysing Experimental Results
QUICK TEST (Page 99)

1. It is used to determine whether a sample set of results is likely to be representative of the true population by determining the probability that the difference between what has been observed and what was expected in an experiment occurred through chance alone.

2. Obs = number observed; Exp = number expected.

3. That there is no difference between the observed and expected values.

4. It is the number of groups minus 1.

5. The Hardy–Weinberg principle states that the allele and genotype frequencies in a population will remain constant from generation to generation, if other evolutionary pressures are absent.

6. $p^2 + 2pq + q^2 = 1$.

7. Frequency of $D = 49\%$, therefore frequency of d must be 51%. ($p^2 = 0.24$, $p = \sqrt{0.24} = 0.49$; $1 - 0.49 = 0.51$).

8. Frequency of dd = $q^2 = 0.51^2 = 0.26$ therefore 26%.

9. $2pq = 2(0.49 \times 0.51) = 50\%$ will be heterozygous Dd.

10. The Hardy–Weinberg principle is disrupted by mutations, natural selection, genetic drift and non-random mating.

PRACTICE QUESTIONS (Page 99)

1. a) **Any two from:** if brown and pink were co-dominant there would be: an extra phenotype/with the heterozygous $S^B S^Y$ snails **[1]**. This is because each allele would be expressed **[1]**. **[2 marks: 1 mark for each point made]**

  b) $S^B S^B$, $S^B S^P$, $S^B S^Y$ **[1]**.

  c) Uses Hardy–Weinberg equation, $p^2 + 2pq + q^2$ **[1]**. $p^2 + 2pq = 0.56$, therefore q^2 is 0.44 (or 56% unbanded, 44% banded, so $q^2 = 0.44$), so q is $\sqrt{0.44}$ or 0.66 **[1]**; p is 0.34, so p^2 is 0.12; $2pq = 2(0.34 \times 0.66)$ is 0.45 **[1]**. Therefore 45% of the population will be heterozygous **[1]**. Answer alone worth 2 marks.

DNA Sequencing
QUICK TEST (Page 102)

1. DNA sequencing.

2. Deoxynucleoside triphosphate.

3. Adenine, thymine, guanine, cytosine.

4. A ddNTP stops replication.

5. … it enables all four nucleotides to be mapped at the same time.

6. DNA from a crime scene is collected and then amplified. Specific variable-number tandem repeats (VNTRs) are mapped and the 'fingerprint' or profile compared to that of the suspect. If they are different then they are likely to be from different individuals; if they are the same it is highly likely to have come from the suspect (unless the suspect has an identical twin).

7. Sequencing is used to identify the relationship between living things, both extant and extinct.

8. Synthetic biology is where the genes have been chosen and inserted into a cell by humans.

9. PCR is the polymerase chain reaction and is a method of amplifying the amount of DNA from a small sample.

10. DNA profiling can be used to identify whether the food is what it says it is, e.g. basmati rice rather than a cheaper type of white rice, or beef rather than horse meat.

PRACTICE QUESTIONS (Page 103)

1. a) TATGACCG **[1]**.

  b) **Any three from:** the modern method uses fluorescent markers attached to each ddNTP; the reaction can be run in one tube rather than four; the results are read by a machine; this speeds up the process/can be automated; and is less dangerous as radioactivity is not involved. **[3 marks: 1 mark for each point made]**

DAY 7

Genetic Engineering
QUICK TEST (Page 106)

1. A restriction endonuclease.
2. It cuts the DNA when a specific DNA nucleotide sequence is present.
3. Plasmids and viruses.
4. The DNA is cut using the same restriction endonuclease and DNA ligase is used to insert the desired gene.
5. Electroporation is where an electric current is used to disrupt the cell surface membrane to allow larger molecules to pass through it.
6. The insulin is human, not of another animal, so vegetarians and vegans can use it as well as those who would have religious issues with pig-derived insulin. The insulin can also be produced in larger quantities.
7. The transferred genes cannot be passed to offspring.
8. Cloning is the creation of genetically identical organisms.
9. Either by embryo twinning (taking an embryo and dividing it into two to form twins) or enucleation followed by somatic cell nuclear transfer (SCNT).
10. As the crop plants are identical there is a greater risk that the entire crop could be wiped out by disease.

PRACTICE QUESTIONS (Page 107)

1. a) **Any two from:** rice is easy to grow/there would not be any need to learn new farming methods; rice forms a major part of the diet/the diet would not need to change; there are a lot of children dying of vitamin A deficiency, this would reduce the number; this would reduce blindness. [**2 marks: 1 mark for each point made**]
   b) **Any three from:** fears about: the rice may reduce genetic variation; the rice may be too expensive; the rice may spread the genes to wild populations; disease may wipe out the entire crop as all plants are the same. [**3 marks: 1 mark for each point made**]
   c) i) Recombinant DNA is DNA that includes a target gene that has come from another organism [1].
      ii) Restriction endonucleases [1].
      iii) DNA ligase [1].

Biotechnology
QUICK TEST (Page 110)

1. Microorganisms grow rapidly and have a short life cycle.
2. There are no ethical barriers to using microorganisms compared to using larger animals such as mammals.
3. Two from: faster protein production compared to plants and animals; production can be easily altered to suit demand; vegetarians can eat the protein.
4. Two from: people may not want to eat products from organisms grown on waste; protein has to be purified to ensure there are no contaminants; the conditions provided are also ideal for pathogens; the texture of protein is different to that of animal and plant protein.
5. Aseptic techniques are used to ensure that no unwanted microorganisms contaminate equipment and nutrient media.

6.

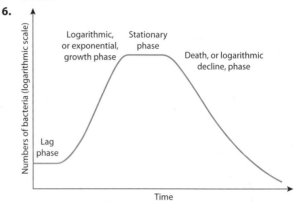

7. Continuous culture is culture using a bioreactor, supplying continual nutrients and removing products before the death or decline phase is reached.
8. A product can be continuously made and extracted.
9. An enzyme is immobilised on to an inert, insoluble support. This may be an inert material (adsorption), covalently bonded, cross-linked in a matrix or encapsulated (trapped inside the support material, e.g. a bead).
10. The enzymes have improved resistance to pH and temperature changes and are easy to remove from the reaction once it has finished.

PRACTICE QUESTIONS (Page 111)

1. a) **Any two from:** immobilised enzymes can tolerate higher temperatures/greater range of pH; enzymes are separate from the product/the product is uncontaminated by enzymes; enzymes are easily added and removed from the reaction. [**2 marks: 1 mark for each point made**]
   b) pH can affect the shape of an enzyme [1]; if the enzyme's shape is altered then it will not work effectively [1].
   c) **Any one from:** attached to an inert material (adsorption); covalently bonded; cross-linked in a matrix. [**1 mark for any point made**]
2. All equipment needs to be sterilised/aseptically treated [1] to ensure no pathogens/unwanted organisms are present [1].

Ecosystems
QUICK TEST (Page 114)

1. An ecosystem is the community of all living organisms in a given area interacting with the abiotic environment.
2. Abiotic factors are the physical and chemical non-living factors.

3. Biotic factors are the living organisms in a habitat.
4. A food chain shows the direction of energy transfer from the producers (autotrophs) to the consumers (heterotrophs).
5. Each stage of a food chain is a different trophic level.
6. $\text{Efficiency} = \dfrac{\text{Biomass transferred to the next level}}{\text{Total biomass in}} \times 100$
7. Humans have altered food chains by farming and hunting of organisms and by changing the biotic and abiotic factors.
8. *Azotobacter* or *Rhizobium*.
9. *Nitrosomonas* spp.
10. Coal and oil are fossilised stores of carbon that, when burned, will release CO_2 into the atmosphere.

PRACTICE QUESTIONS (Page 115)

1. a) **Any two from:** amino acids; protein/named protein; DNA/nucleic acids; urea. **[2 marks: 1 mark for each point made]**
   b) *Azotobacter*, nitrogen fixation/conversion of nitrogen to ammonia **[1]**; *Nitrosomonas*, ammonification/conversion of ammonia to nitrites **[1]**; *Thiobacillus*, denitrification/conversion of nitrate to nitrogen **[1]**.
2. **Any four from:** carbon dioxide is a greenhouse gas; deforestation means less CO_2 removed through photosynthesis; burning/combustion of wood/fossil fuels releases CO_2; farming animals releases methane; methane is a greenhouse gas. **[4 marks: 1 mark for each point made]**

Population Size

QUICK TEST (Page 118)

1. The carrying capacity is the maximum size that a population can reach and sustain indefinitely in a habitat without depleting or degrading the essential resources (e.g. food and water) for that species.
2. As the numbers of prey increase the number of predators increases, leading to a reduction of prey numbers which then leads to a reduction in predators, and so the cycle continues.
3. There will always be pockets of prey that are able to remain hidden from the predators.
4. Intraspecific competition is between members of the same species and interspecific competition is between members of different species.
5. Gause's law of competitive exclusion states that two species competing for exactly the same resources cannot co-exist.
6. Ecosystems are a source of drugs, food and resources, many uses of which have not yet been discovered. If diversity is reduced, these will be lost to future generations.

7. A conserved woodland used for logging would have a plan whereby new trees are replanted continuously to ensure that the woodland does not decrease in size or biodiversity.
8. A preserved area is left to grow and develop without human intervention.
9. Typically lichens and mosses are the first species to colonise newly formed volcanic rock.
10. This is when humans prevent succession from progressing, e.g. by introducing grazing animals that prevent the growth of shrubs and trees.

PRACTICE QUESTIONS (Page 119)

1. a) i) That the species is likely to become extinct/number of individuals is not sustainable/number is too low for the species to survive **[1]**.
      ii) **Any two from:** they are hunted for their coats/other tiger parts/products; their habitat is being destroyed; humans living in Sumatra are fearful of the tiger. **[2 marks: 1 mark for each point made]**
   b) **Any three from:** in captivity the tigers can be monitored by vets; they are protected from poaching; they are protected from habitat loss; funds can be generated from zoo visitors to support the programme. If they were bred *in situ* then there would be a risk that they could still be poached; could die of disease. **[3 marks: 1 mark for each point made]**

Notes

Index

abiotic factors 112
abiotic stress 36
abscission 37
acetylation 81
acetylcholine 25–27
actin 49–50
action potentials 20–21, 24–27
ADH 17–18
adipose cells 73
adrenal glands 28, 30
aerobic respiration 68–71, 72
aldosterone 28
alkaloids 36
alleles 89
alveoli 12
amino acids 12–13, 76–78
anaerobic respiration 73
antigens 5
apical dominance 38, 40–41
apoenzymes 72
apoptosis 84–85
ATP 24, 49–50, 62, 68–71
ATP synthase 62, 69–71
auxins 37–38, 40–43

bacteria 104–105, 108–109, 113–114
biodiversity 116–117
biomass transfers 112–113
biotechnology 108–111
biotic factors 112
biotic stresses 36–37
blood vessels 9–10, 13
bone 52–59
Bowman's capsule 16–17
brain anatomy 44–47

calcium deficiency 53
Calvin cycle 64
cancer 81–82
carbon cycle 114
carbon dioxide 64–65, 114
cardiac muscle 50
carrying capacity 113, 116
cartilage 52, 57
cell junctions 4–5
cell recognition 4–5
cell signalling 4–7, 48
chemiosmotic theory 72
chi-squared (χ^2) test 96–97
chlorophyll 60–61
chloroplasts 60–67
cholinergic synapses 25–27

chondrocytes 52
chromosomes 88–91
cloning 105–106
codominance 89
coenzymes 72
competition 116
cone cells 22
conservation 117
cortisol 28
counter-current flow 17
creatine phosphate 50
cristae 68–70
culturing 105, 108–109

deamination 12
decomposers 114
denitrification 114
depolarisation 24–25
desmosomes 50
diabetes 33–35
dialysis 18
dihybrid inheritance 88–91
diploid 88–91
displaced fractures 56
DNA 76–77, 80–84, 100–105
DNA ligase 104–105
DNA profiling 101
DNA sequencing 100–103

ecosystems 112–119
effectors 8–11, 20, 48–51
electroporation 104–105
embryo twinning 105
embryonic development 84–87
encapsulation 109–110
endocrine system 5, 28–35
endosymbiosis 60
enucleation 105–106
enzymes 72–75, 85, 100–101, 104–105, 109–110
epigenetics 81
epistasis 89
ethylene 37, 42
eukaryotic cells 68
evolution 94, 97–98
excretion 12–19
exons 81
eyes 21–22

FAD/FADH$_2$ 69, 72–73
fermentation 73
flowering 37

fluid balance 37–38
food production 108–109
founder effect 93
fovea 22
fractures 56
fruit ripening 42

Gause's law of competitive exclusion 116
gene duplication 77
gene expression 80–87
gene therapy 105
genetic bottlenecks 93
genetic code 76–77
genetic drift 93
genetic engineering 104–107
genetic profiling 101
genetics 76–107
geotropism 41
germination 37, 40–41
gibberellins 37–38, 41
glucagon 29, 33–35
gluconeogenesis 14
glucose 8, 14, 29, 32–35, 64, 73–74
glycogen 14, 33
glycolysis 68–69
grey matter 45

Hardy–Weinberg principle 97–98
Haversian system 53
hepatocytes 13
histones 81
holoenzymes 72–75
homeobox genes 84
homeostasis 8–11, 17–18, 29, 32–35
hormones 5, 17–18, 28–43, 45–46
Hox genes 84
hydroxyapatite 53
hypothalamus 44–47

immobilised enzymes 109–110
inheritance 88–91
insulin 29, 32–35
intercalated disks 50
interphase 84
introns 81
involuntary muscles 50
islets of Langerhans 29, 32–33
isolating mechanisms 94

joints 56–58

kidneys 16–19, 28
Krebs cycle 69
kyphosis 57

lactic acid 73
legumes 113
light-dependent stage 61–62
light detection 21–22
light-harvesting systems 61
light-independent stage 64–67
limiting factors 64–65
link reaction 69
lipids 73–74
liver 13–14, 33
loop of Henle 17

matrix 68
mechanical responses 36–37
metabolic reactions 76–78
methylation 81
microorganism culture 108–109
mitochondria 68–71
mitosis 84–85
monogenic inheritance 88
mRNA 76, 81
muscles 48–51
mutations 76–79, 82
myelination 21, 24–25
myofibrils 49–50
myosin 49–50

NAD$^+$/NADH$_2$ 68–69, 72–73
NADP/NADPH$_2$ 61–62, 64
natural selection 92–93
negative feedback 8–11, 32–33
nephrons 16–19
nervous system 5, 20–27, 44–47
neurohormones 45–46
neurones 5, 20–27, 44–45
next-generation sequencing 100–101
nitrogen cycle 113–114
nitrogen metabolism 12–13
nodes of Ranvier 21, 24–25
non-channel synapses 26
null hypothesis 96–97

oncogenes 82
operons 80
ornithine cycle 12–13
osmoreceptors 17–18
osmosis 37–38
osteoblasts/osteoclasts 53
osteomalacia 53–54

osteoporosis 54, 57
oxidative phosphorylation 69–70
Pacinian corpuscles 20–21
pancreas 29–30, 32–33
paracrine signalling 5
perichondrium 52
perimysium 48–49
phenotypes 85
phenylketonuria 77–78
pheromones 36
photomorphogenesis 37
photosynthesis 60–67, 114
phototropism 40–41
phylogenetic trees 100–101
pigments 22, 60–61
pioneer species 118
plant experiments 40–43
plant signalling 5, 36–43
plant tissue culture 105
plasmodesmata 4–5
polymerase chain reaction 101–102
populations 97–98, 116–119
porins 68
positive feedback 8–9
post-transcriptional regulation 81
post-translational modification 81
posterior pituitary 46
predator–prey relationships 116
preservation 117
primers 100
prokaryotes 4, 104–105, 108, 113–114
proteases 85
proteome 76
protocells 101
proximal convoluted tubule 17
Punnett squares 88–89, 97
pyruvate 68–69, 73

receptors 5, 8–11, 17–18, 25–27, 33
recombinant DNA 104
recycling 113
redundancy 76
reflexes 44–45
refractory period 25
regulation 8–11, 80–83
repressor proteins 80
respiration 12, 68–75, 114
respiratory quotients 74
resting potentials 24
restriction enzymes 100–101, 104–105
retina 22
rhodopsin 22
ribulose bisphosphate 64

rickets 53–54
RNA 76, 81
RNA interference 81
rod cells 22
rooting powders 42
Rubisco 64

sarcomeres 49–50
Schwann cells 21
scoliosis 57
second messengers 48
seeds 37, 40–41
selective reabsorption 17
sex linkage 89–90
signalling 4–7, 5, 20–27, 28–43, 36–43, 48
skeletal muscle 48–51
skeletal tissues 52–59
skeleton 56–59
smooth muscle 50
sodium-potassium pumps 24
speciation 94
spine 45, 56–57
standard deviation 96
stem elongation 38, 41
stomata 37–38
striated muscle 49–50
succession 118
summation 26
synapses 5, 25–27
synovial joints 57
synthetic biology 101

thylakoids 60–63
tissue culture 105
trans-acting proteins 81
transcription factors 80–81
triose phosphate 64
tropism 36, 38, 40–43

ultrafiltration 17
urine 12–13, 16

variation 85, 92–98
vasoconstriction/vasodilation 9–10
vectors 104–105
veins 13
vertebrae 56–57
vitamin D deficiency 53–54

water 17–18, 37–38, 65
white matter 45

Acknowledgements

The author and publisher are grateful to the copyright holders for permission to use quoted materials and images.

Cover & P1: © Shutterstock.com/MADDRAT

All other images are © Shutterstock.com and © HarperCollins*Publishers* Ltd

Every effort has been made to trace copyright holders and obtain their permission for the use of copyright material. The author and publisher will gladly receive information enabling them to rectify any error or omission in subsequent editions. All facts are correct at time of going to press.

Published by Letts Educational
An imprint of HarperCollins*Publishers*
1 London Bridge Street
London SE1 9GF

ISBN: 9780008179076

First published 2016

10 9 8 7 6 5 4 3 2 1

© HarperCollins*Publishers* Limited 2016

British Library Cataloguing in Publication Data.
A CIP record of this book is available from the British Library.

Series Concept and Development: Emily Linnett and Katherine Wilkinson
Commissioning and Series Editor: Chantal Addy
Author: Eliot Attridge
Project Manager and Editorial: Nik Prowse
Cover Design: Paul Oates
Inside Concept Design: Paul Oates and Ian Wrigley
Index: Simon Yapp
Text Design, Layout and Artwork: Q2A Media
Production: Lyndsey Rogers and Paul Harding
Printed in Italy by Grafica Veneta SpA

MIX
Paper from
responsible sources
FSC™ C007454